GOOD INTENTIONS

GOOD INTENTIONS

The Nine Unconscious Mistakes
of Nice People

DUKE ROBINSON

WARNER BOOKS

A Time Warner Company

Warner Books, Inc., 1271 Avenue of the Americas, New York, N.Y. 10020

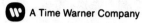 A Time Warner Company

Printed in the United States of America
First printing: July 1997

10   9   8   7   6   5   4   3   2   1

Library of Congress Cataloging-in-Publication Data

Robinson, Duke.
    Good intentions : the nine unconscious mistakes of nice people /
Duke Robinson.
        p. cm.
    ISBN 0-446-52085-3
    1. Self-defeating behavior.   2. Self-management (Psychology)
I. Title.
BF637.S37R63   1997
158'.1—dc20   96-34866
                                                    CIP

Book design and composition by L&G McRee

To Barbara,
   with whom I have worked on my "niceness" for
   more than forty years of marriage, whose separate
   sense of self allowed both of us to survive the
   writing of this book, and to whom I owe so much
   more than I am able to see or appreciate.

To Margo, Andrew, Steve, and Stuart,
   our grown children, who are their own persons in
   spite of any nice behaviors we modeled while they
   were young, whom we love very much, and whose
   love and families bring us much joy.

Acknowledgments

Some insights in this book emerged decades ago as I pursued my formal education. Others came over nearly forty years of reading, teaching, counseling, and leading seminars on human consciousness and behavior. Some of these sources are lost from memory. A few that I've retained stand out.

I trace the key phrase *accepting your acceptance* to Harvard theologian Paul Tillich, certain ideas found in the second chapter to time-management expert Alan Lakein, the "I" message paradigm in the fourth chapter to Thomas Gordon and his book *Parent Effectiveness Training*, the five steps in the grief process listed in the ninth chapter to the death and dying pioneer Elisabeth Kübler-Ross, and the radical distinction between protecting and supporting the bereaved, also in that chapter, to fellow clergyman William Sloan Coffin. I acknowledge my debt to these creative thinkers.

For twenty-eight years, until July 1996, I served as pastor of the Montclair Presbyterian Church of Oakland, California. All that time it provided me a loving and intellectually stimulating community. It also granted the sabbaticals that enabled me to get this book off the ground. I am deeply grateful for these gifts.

My church staff colleagues were most supportive as I put the book together, especially John Hadsell, our Theologian in Residence, whose encouragement and literary criticism proved invaluable. Our secretary, Judy Fletcher, handled my copying needs efficiently. I deeply appreciate their contributions.

I also want to thank a contract group at the church that met with me for ten sessions in 1992 to discuss the behaviors I cover in this book and critique some of my earliest drafts: Doug Ferguson, Bill Ferrier, Margot Lyon, Eloise Gilland, Lloyd and Rita Perry, Marjorie Rawls, Raphael Shevalev, Linda Streb, and Jack York.

I am grateful, too, to friends Mimi Loyd, Polly Orr, and Dave Rudd, who reviewed the manuscript at various stages. And to Vern and Gloria Alexander, Hazel Angell, John Barr, Janet Clyde, Dale and Elsie Cooper, Robin Crawford, Parry Dent, Karen Flamme, Eleanor Gertmenian, Virginia Hadsell, Louise Hermanson, Robert Hirni, David Hyde, Sally Juarez, Wally Kelly, Minda Lucero, Marna McKenzie, Joy Palmerlee, Norm and Enid Pott, Dean and Dorothy Skanderup, David Vandre, and Guy Wulfing, all of whom, at various times, offered support or constructive criticism related to their personal experience or professional expertise.

I want to thank my literary agent, Laurie Harper of the Sebastian Agency, San Francisco, who both affirmed the book's strengths and told me what simply wouldn't do. Her savvy, moxie, and the widespread respect she enjoys from major publishing houses had a lot to do with getting the book into print. I also couldn't have done without her personal and professional attention that prepared me to face the sometimes terrifying publishing process.

My special thanks also go to Susan Suffes, my editor at Warner Books, who believed in this book immediately and whose care and professional skill helped make it better. I am deeply grateful for her availability, great energy, and support as she carefully led me, step by step, through the publishing labyrinth.

Many unnamed people helped give shape to this book. Some of them don't know it. Some of them I can't identify. I offer them, whoever and wherever they are, my heartfelt appreciation.

Contents

Introduction

You are a *nice person*. You always try to do what others expect. While you'll do anything for them, you never ask a thing for yourself. You're careful not to hurt others' feelings or blow your top. When irrationally attacked, you remain reasonable and calm. You're always ready to offer good advice. Although a friend's drinking embarrasses you, you would never think of embarrassing her. And you never talk of Grandpa's death in front of Grandma. **You are a *really nice person*.**

Sometime back in the mid-sixties, I sat in my office late one night listening to a nice young man talk about himself and the woman he planned to marry. He loved her and couldn't bear the thought of hurting her, but she constantly expected things from him that made him angry. And every time he felt this way, what he did either made matters worse between them or made him feel untrue to himself. For most of the hour he vacillated between giving up on this relationship and resolving to do better at what he had been doing, even though he knew it wasn't working. He felt confused and lost. And so did I.

Driving home that night, I thought of the other nice people whose stories I had heard recently: a widow who never said no to her friends and was all burned out; a middle-aged man who could never be honest with people who disappointed him or wanted more from him than he could offer; a woman who could never please her bedridden mother and didn't have the faintest idea how to talk with her.

I remember having two reactions as I slipped into bed. First, I thought, These are really nice people. They're smart, they have good intentions, their values are sound, they want to live productive lives, they're not crazy. But they constantly waste their time and undermine their best interests by what they say and do.

Second, I said to myself for the very first time, That's exactly what I do. I am one of these really nice people.

I knew before then that I tried too hard to impress other people with what a nice person I was. I also saw that some of my socially acceptable behaviors sometimes got in the way of my good intentions. But I had not realized the extent to which being a nice person dominated and damaged my approaches to work and relationships. My eyes were beginning to open to the negative impact niceness had on my life.

These reflections drove me to look more honestly at how being a nice person affected me. With a new awareness, I began to identify more of my self-defeating behaviors: I regularly said yes to people when I should have said no; I consistently cut myself off from others by not telling them what I wanted, by pretending I was calm when I was angry and by lying whenever I was afraid to hurt their feelings; and time and time again I frustrated myself by taking responsibility for the problems of those I cared about.

I became aware of this last behavior through another conversation that made an impression on me. Several psychologists and social workers, along with a number of my colleagues and I, began meeting weekly with a renowned psychiatrist to reflect on how we operated as members of the helping professions. At one session the doctor suggested that for us to jump on our horses and dash off to save people who had problems was damaging to both them and us. He caught me by surprise. I'd never thought seriously about that. I was trained in pastoral counseling and was gaining experience, but I had always assumed that in the normal traffic of everyday living, nice people—particularly those in my profession—should try to save everyone they can.

Again it hit me: **We nice people constantly undermine our good intentions.**

I started talking informally to colleagues and friends about these kinds of behaviors. Soon we were acknowledging how painful it was to think about rejection and how it drove us relentlessly to please those who were important to us. We shared how difficult it was to express our strong feelings, particularly our anger, and how this derailed our communication and put distance between us and those we loved. We talked, too, of how stymied we usually were in our efforts to straighten others out or help them solve their problems.

I became increasingly curious about these behaviors. Where did they come from and why did we act this way? Why were they so damaging? What would it take for us to stop sabotaging our good intentions and act differently?

I also became eager to develop theory and practice that would enable me and other nice people to stop acting in these ways. So I went back to basic sources in psychology, theology, and the behavioral sciences, and drew upon some of the more thoughtful literature of the human-potential movement. From these studies and continued consultations with other professionals, helpful insights into alternative behaviors for nice people began to emerge. As they did, I tested them on myself and introduced the more effective ones to my seminars and counseling sessions. Over the past several decades, these alternative ways of acting have proved helpful to a large number of people, including me. They became real as we were willing to deal with our stressful lives, our bottled-up feelings, our fear of emotionally loaded social encounters, and our failed attempts to be helpful to others. They continue to liberate us from a sense of personal failure and a great deal of frustration and dissatisfaction. They also empower the pages that follow.

THE MISTAKES OF NICE PEOPLE

In a sad, ironic twist our *niceness* betrays us. Call it one of life's little jokes. We sincerely want to make the most of our lives, to be close to those who are important to us, and to feel satisfied whenever we try to help others;

we abound with good intentions. Yet whenever we talk and act in the nice ways we were taught—and that almost everyone accepts as normal—we are left feeling worn out, unsure of ourselves, and frustrated.

In this book, I refer to these behaviors as *mistakes*. They are not as heavy, as debilitating, or as dark as, say, psychoses or phobias or character disorders. So while I examine psychological dimensions of these behaviors, I am not offering psychotherapy for emotional illness or prescribing quick-fix solutions for complex inner conflicts. I am simply addressing things we well-intentioned, nice people routinely do that adversely affect our relationships and take the luster from our lives. Day after day they get in our way, drive us crazy, and steal precious time and energy from our most important endeavors. They boil down to nine self-defeating mistakes that are worthy of our attention because with relatively little insight and effort we can stop making them.

As you will see, I make no distinction between how women and men make these mistakes. I realize the sexes tend to approach social encounters differently and from different perspectives. I also know that either gender may be more prone to make certain of these mistakes, that women usually suffer more social pressure than men to be nice, and that most people think that men tend not to be as nice as women. But whether you are a nice woman or a nice man, chances are you repeatedly make these nine mistakes in all your relationships, to your own detriment.

A key to understanding these mistakes is insight into niceness itself.

NICENESS ITSELF

Our parents, with good intentions, raised us to get along with our siblings, to have lots of friends, and to grow into persons who will be civil and socially acceptable. For the most part, they did not groom us to be insipid or saccharine sweet, but considerate, courteous, and always helpful to those who are in need. In other words, to be nice. Accordingly, they taught us—supported by our teachers and perhaps by authorities in religion—to do what we are told and to do it well, to be passive rather than pushy, and to find deep satisfaction in helping others solve their problems.

As we moved through childhood, their teachings and models of niceness—which we began to mimic unconsciously—planted strong messages in the back of our minds. These messages not only dictated how we operated in our earliest years, but became recorded memories that established themselves as our internal critics, our unconscious *guardians of niceness*. So even today, the moment we make contact with others, there are voices inside our heads saying things like:

Whatever is worth doing is worth doing well.
Always say yes to a friend.
Don't be selfish.
Never lose your cool.
Be reasonable.
Don't say anything to hurt others' feelings.
Help your friends with their problems.
Be thoughtful of those in pain.
Always be nice.

OUR NICENESS MISTAKES DAMAGE US

First, we must acknowledge that not everything about being nice is bad. For one thing, it means we are sensitive to the needs of family and friends, and psychologists tell us that those who are considerate of others are healthier and happier than selfish people. For another thing, niceness saves us from criticism, embarrassment, and rejection, and whenever we are nice, other nice people invariably think we're wonderful. Moreover, consideration and courtesy pave the way for the creation of a humane society and help make this world a bit more civil and bearable. On rare but not unimportant occasions, niceness spurs some people to be courageous, even heroic. Thus in many ways our nice behaviors serve us well. And it's this positive side to them that we admire and like to think about.

The problem is that they also collect negative tolls and cost us a lot more than we bargain for. The first two mistakes, which are related—trying to be perfect and taking on too much—drive us to exhaustion. They weigh us down so we feel like overloaded ships that are listing and sinking. I begin with these two mistakes, by the way, for three reasons: (1) They are among the toughest of the nine to avoid; (2) the need that fuels our inclination to make them causes us to some degree to make all the other seven; and (3) if we can cease making them, we will have more energy to tackle the others.

The next four mistakes—not saying what you want, suppressing your anger, reasoning with irrationality, and telling little lies—cost us real measures of our integrity because we lose touch with our emotional sides. We all agree that our feelings are important to our interactions with others. But when our feelings don't fit our niceness (e.g., we desire something, we're angry with someone, or we're afraid of losing control), we stifle them; we actually teach ourselves not to feel. Sometimes we push them so deep inside we don't know they're there, or we can't locate them. If they break out or we track them down, we often find we can't handle their intensity or size. So we go through the motions of emotional transactions generally ignorant of our feelings, denying them, hiding them, or mired down in them and stressed out, mainly because we're afraid. Indeed, it's fear of our emotions that most often holds us hostage, causing us to pretend we don't feel what we do. And as a result, we fail to experience authentic closeness both with ourselves and with those who are important to us.

The last three mistakes—giving advice, rescuing others, and protecting those in grief—cause us to subvert the interests of the people we want to help and often make their problems worse. We have no better conscious intention than to be helpful, but because these behaviors are unconscious attempts to control others while making us look and feel good, they invalidate themselves from the start.

We originally adopted these nine behaviors to be socially acceptable, to avoid emotional pain, and to help those in need. And, at first, engaging in them made us feel good about ourselves. We continue them today out of habit, because they seem normal to us and because we often don't even recognize their sometimes dreadful consequences. Yes, a few of them drive us crazy. But even when they do, we tend not to see them as problems for which we're responsible. And if we do see them as such, we're usually too busy to give much thought to how we can stop repeating them. Moreover, deep down, far from our awareness, we're afraid that if we stop behaving in these ways, we may no longer be nice people.

THE NEED TO CHANGE

It's important to see that as nice people we have been trained by a well-meaning but misguided molding of our minds—we have been programmed with consciousness-controlling messages that misdirect our behavior. It also is critical to understand that we do not have to feel forever sorry for ourselves or always be blaming our problems on our parents—we are not helpless victims of heredity and early family life. Moreover, it helps to know that these misdirections are not unique to you and me—they are extremely common. And further, we do not need to keep plowing the same self-defeating ruts—there are specific ways to avoid them. By putting these nine mistakes behind us and acting on new descriptions of who we are and how we can behave, you and I can reshape the present and transform what our futures will be. With a little awareness and effort we can change ourselves in ways that will make us so much more whole than we've ever been.

It is equally important to understand that the changes I am talking about do not require us to stop being nice. Instead, they ask us to affirm the value of our good intentions and society's standards, even as we reclaim what we've lost of ourselves and begin to act differently. They call us to balance our niceness with genuineness. To make these changes we must learn to (1) view ourselves through new eyes; (2) process our feelings directly and sensitively; and (3) assist others in ways that respect their freedom and provide the genuine help they need. To do this, we must change our inner messages. And yes, this means we must have the courage to disobey our parents.

HOW THIS BOOK WILL HELP YOU

In each chapter I describe one of the mistakes nice people make, then explain why we make it and why it's important to give it up. Of course, to understand what is wrong—and even to stop doing it—is usually not enough. So along with each mistake, you'll see a life-affirming behavior you can put in its place, and in each chapter I'll demonstrate effective ways to stop making the former and adopt the latter. But even as the insights you encounter here ring true and promise to be helpful, you are the one who must decide to apply them; you are the one who must make them move from these pages and become real for you.

This book assumes that we all make these mistakes in a myriad of daily social transactions marked by complexity, unpredictability, and social risk. In each alternative behavior, therefore, there is a series of possible steps to take in a dynamic, somewhat open process. You can be, therefore, flexible about which steps to take, when, and in what order. For example, you don't always have to start with step number one. On occasion, you may want to skip a step or two, depending on when you enter the situation and on how serious it is. Sometimes you may need to repeat one particular step several times. But once you master the steps in these processes, you'll possess the skills to make up appropriate responses in each situation as you go along.

As a result of learning these skills, each of us will be able to

- Liberate ourselves from bondage to others' expectations.
- Say no when appropriate, and save ourselves from overload.
- Tell others what we want from them and actually receive it.
- Express our anger in ways that heal and maintain our relationships.
- Respond effectively when people irrationally criticize or attack us.
- Tell the truth to friends when they fail us.
- Care for others without the burden of trying to run their lives.
- Help self-destructive friends and loved ones to recover.
- Feel competent and helpful in the presence of pain and grief.

You can change. I changed, as you'll see through the stories in this book. Change will not always be easy and immediate and, no, you won't become perfect. You will not be immune to the unwanted surprises and ongoing difficulties of life, and certain of these habits may trouble you as long as you live. But you'll also be surprised at the progress you make and the habits you break. And as you successfully negotiate social transactions that used to be so defeating, you'll respect yourself as a more competent person, you'll feel closer to those you care about, and you'll find that you are genuinely effective in support of others.

And you'll still be a *nice person*.

Mistake #1
TRYING TO BE PERFECT

> While writing to a friend on routine matters, you misspell a word on page two, so you start all over. Halfway through a second draft, you notice smudges on page one, so you begin again. As you go to sign draft three, you realize that twice you have ended a sentence with a preposition. So you rewrite two pages. This unimportant letter to a friend has taken a prime-time hour. And you're annoyed at yourself.

Much of my professional work was public and had performance dimensions to it, including a lot of up-front public speaking. From the start, I felt vulnerable to criticism, not only for not being clever or entertaining enough, but also for making simple mistakes. Someone has said that criticism doesn't bother him unless it's from a stranger, an acquaintance, a co-worker, a friend, or a family member. That's exactly the way I felt.

1

One evening, back in the late fifties when I was still wet behind the ears professionally, I was teaching a large class of adults and used the word *perplexion* in reference to the state of being perplexed. Afterward, a mentor of mine told me in front of another colleague—while smirking—that there is no such word as *perplexion* (the word is *perplexity*). Because he was right, it cut straight to the bone. Today a mistake like that wouldn't bother me as it did then. But whenever I remember that moment, I can feel the hurt again.

In those early years, I was mostly unaware of how excessive my efforts to be perfect sometimes were. Whenever I couldn't help but see how much strain I put on myself, I tried to ignore it. For too long, I wasted a lot of time and energy carefully guarding my reputation as a nice person and a competent professional. It was several years before I saw how liberating it could be to accept my shortcomings and live with the fact that I wasn't perfect and never would be.

Nobody's perfect. We all know this. But as nice people, we feel the constant pressure to do things exactly the way they *should* be done every single time. We also demand that certain people always perform perfectly on their jobs—airline pilots, brain surgeons, bridge builders, and umpires come to mind. And while we would all like to be perfect at everything, the things we do well or think are most important are given our best shot. As a result, our successes in accomplishment and performance not only make us feel special, they also enable us to reach some of our highest goals. So you often appreciate what your perfectionism does for you.

But you've lived long enough with the pressure your perfectionism generates to know it burdens you and, ironically, often bothers those around you. You may not fully understand why you engage in your perfectionism or see it as totally bad, but you very likely know you would be relieved if you could stop practicing it.

UNDERSTANDING PERFECTIONISM AS SOCIAL

To stop being perfectionists, it's important to know we are social by nature and perfectionism is a social matter. We are social in that we can fulfill important facets of our personalities only in relationship with others. Yes, we are individual persons, but we cannot be whole by ourselves in isolation. The healthy, true self is the self-in-community.

To see yourself as a self-in-community is to realize that your finest moments are in concert with others— working on tasks, dancing, playing team sports, performing in a play or playing in an orchestra, reading a book someone else has written, going to a picnic, or partying. As an individual, you can experience or accomplish something for your own, sheer satisfaction. But for it to take on full meaning, you must share it with others. Stand in rapture before the most beautiful sunset you've ever seen and you have to tell family and friends about it. Receive an award, complete the biggest sale of the year, hit a home run, or bake a beautiful blueberry pie; if those important to you never hear of it, you feel lonely, incomplete, even cheated.

We also are social in that other people inhabit us. You are a dynamic community made up of all those who directly or indirectly have touched your life in positive or negative ways. Whether they are living or dead, they dwell in you by their continuing influence and through your conscious and unconscious memories of them.

We are social, too, in that we did not create ourselves. It was our families, friends, and the world-at-large who taught us to become persons, to think, to create, to use language and develop our native skills as members of society. They also gave us the standards by which we continue to judge human values, behavior, and achievement. Were it not for these standards, we could not begin to conceive of what we ought to expect of ourselves.

And here's where perfectionism comes in: We strive to be perfect to meet the standards set for us by others, the others who enable us to complete our lives through relationship, the others who dwell inside of us by influence, the others to whom we are inextricably linked as humans. In the end, trying to be perfect is the unconscious social effort to **please** *ourselves* **by pleasing these** *others*.

PERFECTIONISM AND SOCIAL ACCEPTANCE

The social power that drives our perfectionism and, therefore, the power we must transcend or transform to be free from it, is our profound need to be accepted. Because we have been trained to be nice, this need dominates our every waking moment, causing us to approach almost everything we do so that people who are important to us will be impressed enough to take us to themselves and never let us go. Rather than being taught to accept ourselves, we were trained to make ourselves socially acceptable. And whenever we fail, we suffer inside.

- Fred meets three friends of his boss at a party, and ten seconds later he realizes he can't remember their names. He then spends a terrifying five minutes trying to get away from them without embarrassing himself.
- Before Jennifer serves dinner to her husband's large office staff, she calls a dozen stores to ask about less expensive wines. After dinner she overhears one guest whisper to another, "No one serves white zinfandel anymore." The whole evening is ruined.
- Ted works hard on a speech to colleagues, several of whom go out of their way to say it was helpful. But all he can think about is that he fumbled the opening anecdote, and he can't shake it for a week.
- Cleo likes the new man she's met, and hears he likes women who are super thin. So she starves herself, lifts weights, and sweats aerobics six days a week for two months. And a friend now tells her he is seeing someone who is pleasantly plump.

Psychologists tell us that our parents play the primary role in giving our powerful drive for acceptance such control over us. No matter how they treated us as children or how radical our adolescent break from them was—and even if they are not alive today—our exhausting search for acceptance may be our attempt to recapture the connection we first cherished in their arms as infants. We also may be driven by warm memories of approval by a parent, teacher, coach, or favorite uncle for something we achieved. On the other hand, if childhood memories are about ridicule and rejection, or even unrealistic expectations and criticism, we may be trying to erase the awful pain buried in those recollections and find the healing reception we never enjoyed.

Whether our early history was positive or negative, we all have the basic human need to know we're acceptable as valid human beings. Unfortunately, this natural longing, which springs from our relational nature as social animals, has been deepened and distorted by our training to be nice. As a result, these dominating powers—nature and niceness—combine to create an anxiety in us that predisposes us to be perfectionists and presume: If only I can please the people I admire, they will accept me. And I will be happy.

The desire for acceptance is normal and understandable. But our training in niceness makes us think that to be acceptable and accepted we must never fail to impress those who are important to us. We carry in our minds the image of that undefined, wonderful person we think society and our parents have told us we must be in order to be accepted and successful. And so we work relentlessly to keep proving ourselves to them in order to secure our acceptance. And in the end, commitment to this tireless effort becomes the most significant mistake we make that stands in the way of our knowing wholeness and joy.

WHY PERFECTIONISM IS A MISTAKE

Nice people don't stop to examine the reality that perfectionism:

- Is a foolish, futile attempt to do the impossible.
- Creates undue anxiety and turns our stress into distress.
- Makes us feel like dying when we make a mistake.
- Causes us to waste precious time and energy.
- Retards the development of close friendships.
- Makes us resent the very people we try so hard to please.
- Can lead to a variety of life-threatening diseases.
- Drives us to excesses that are never satisfying.
- Makes us feel stupid and become overbearing self-blamers.
- Lets others run our lives, which is unfair to them and to us.

This last point needs to be stressed. It is not up to others to run our lives. It is *our* privilege and *our* burden. While it is appropriate for society to set standards and for others to express their opinions, it is not fitting for us to let them define our lives or dictate everything we do. When we let others control us by the threat of disapproval and rejection, we give up far too much of ourselves and make it impossible for us to engage in authentic relationships.

But be clear about this: It is not a mistake to use either your own or society's standards for achievement and strive for excellence. **Trying to be perfect is a mistake only when:**

- You are consumed with keeping your social image untainted.
- You are not prepared or suited to meet what others expect of you.
- It dictates how you approach every little thing you do.
- It pushes you to set unrealistic standards for yourself.
- Tasks cost more in time, energy, money, or worry than they're worth.
- You give up your own growth to please those who don't care about you.
- Failure and disapproval rob you of well-deserved satisfaction for your effort.
- You waste precious time trying to be perfect, rather than spending your time on real priorities.
- It causes you to compromise your values and ideals.
- You have to take alcohol or other drugs to cover how you feel about your imperfections.
- You never please yourself or those who are important to you.
- Your relentless striving damages your emotional or physical health.
- You end up resenting what you are doing.

It's important to know, too, that it is your responsibility to stop submitting to your perfectionism. Society and certain people may have imposed their standards on you, but if they continue to control how you behave, it is you who allows it. Moreover, others are not going to save you from your perfectionism. Only *you* can do that.

DECIDING TO STOP YOUR PERFECTIONISM

But how can you break its power? Where do you begin?

You can begin with your power of decision. It is one of your most valuable resources. There are two steps to take immediately.

STEP ONE: DECIDE THAT ALWAYS TRYING TO BE PERFECT IS A MISTAKE

Until you come to terms with your perfectionism as a self-defeating mistake, you will not want to change. Until you want to change you will continue striving to please others. Say to yourself: **"Living essentially to please others is a monumental mistake."** Say it over and over, meditate on it, or write it out several times until it becomes a part of you.

STEP TWO: DECIDE TO STOP MAKING THIS MISTAKE

This sounds simplistic, but until you actually commit to stop doing something, you remain stuck in thought and theory. It's not enough to appreciate the fact that perfectionism is a mistake. To break the habit you must make the *choice* not to do it any longer. And while the choice itself is not the same as reaching your destination, it is the important first step in the right direction.

AN ALTERNATIVE TO ALWAYS PLEASING OTHERS

If you've made this choice to stop trying to be perfect, you now must find a different way to run your life.

It's important to understand immediately that you cannot flip-flop from always pleasing others to always pleasing yourself. This is another mistake, another tyranny. You are not looking for the freedom to do what you *want* to do, **because what you want to do is not always in your best interest.** (You may want a second chocolate truffle, but your best interest is in being healthy and losing fifteen pounds.) What you are looking for is a freedom that will save you from lapsing back into perfectionism by liberating you to express the best of yourself and serve your deepest interests. This freedom will enable you to choose when to try to be perfect and when not to, when to strive for excellence and when to take it easy, when to do what you need to do, even when others won't like it.

This is genuine freedom.

Such freedom is based on very different understandings of reality from those that underpin your niceness and perfectionism. To experience it, therefore, you must trade the views you were originally taught for truths that reflect your basic social nature and liberate you from the overpowering need to please others. In the same way that flat-earth people during the Renaissance were forced to see the planet in a radically different way, so nice people today—if they are to transform themselves for genuine freedom and integrity—must adopt different views of human life than those society gave them when they were children. The point is that the ideas you embrace make a difference as to how you live: They matter, because if they correspond to what is real, they have the power to set you free. In the end, therefore, freedom isn't something you stumble over or that somebody gives you; it's something you carefully claim, nurture, and protect.

Of course, knowledge of important truths by itself does not effect personal freedom and transformation. Loyalty to truth is required also. You experience freedom not simply when you understand truths you know are necessary for your well-being, but when you obligate yourself to certain actions that reflect those truths. You take on such obligations—perhaps after resisting and struggling with them for a long time—because you come to see them as laws of life that you cannot break without breaking yourself. And even though you know that obeying these laws may not bring you immediate pleasure, you are convinced deep down that they will enrich you and that not to live by them is to betray yourself. At the same time, you know that no arbitrary authority can compel you to obey them. You alone must choose to do that.

This alternative to perfectionism, which is worth embracing because it can free you to serve your own deepest interests, requires your loyalty to three basic understandings:

1. The Psychology of Interdependence

When we were children the inner dynamic that tied us to everything else was *dependence.* We were dependent on our parents, family, neighbors, schools, and the larger community for just about everything. Our very survival rested in their hands. In our teen years we wrested our lives from adult authority in general and parental power in particular to take our chances with *independence*—we tried to depend on ourselves for just about everything. Psychologically, we shifted from one extreme to the other. Ideally, as we entered adulthood, we left behind both childhood dependence and adolescent independence and made our way to the middle ground of *interdependence,* to the interactive balance of dependence and independence that means maturity and wholeness.

Both niceness and perfectionism perpetuate the psychology of dependence. They downplay your rights and power, and play up the power of other people to control you. They suspend your rightful interests and subordinate them to the interests of others. They place your emotional and psychological well-being in the hands of everyone but you.

The authentic freedom I've talked about, on the other hand, thrives on your rights as an adult and on the adult psychology of interdependence. It is grounded in the fact you're designed to be both dependent and independent at the same time. Such interdependence affirms your social nature by calling you to mutuality, equality, and justice for everyone, including you. Thus, to be liberated from perfectionism, you must undergo a shift **from dependence to interdependence;** you must honor yourself as an adult who stands on your own two feet and takes responsibility for your life, all the while recognizing how much others can contribute to it. If you are going to maintain freedom from perfectionism, you must learn to operate interdependently, to develop an adult psychological style.

2. THE ETHIC OF THE COMMON GOOD

The notion of living for the common good was a central concern of our nation's founders. It has been replaced today in most people's minds by the ethic that tells you to live first of all for your own good. In contrast, the earlier American ethic of the common good calls you to serve first the worlds of those who surround you and those who dwell inside you, so that everyone benefits, including yourself. (We'll deal with the legitimacy of self-interest later.)

This ethic stands on a positive paradox, one of those important, apparent contradictions that surprisingly and happily turns out to be true. It says: Live to serve what is good for all—rather than simply what is good for you—and you serve yourself. For example, give time to an environmental group working in your community to promote recycling or reduce industrial pollution, and you not only create a safer, healthier place in which to live, but you also enjoy the deep satisfaction of doing something important with others. To set your life in line with this ethic enriches you and contributes to your wholeness.

It is not surprising that this form of self-sacrifice leads to self-fulfillment. It encourages you to be true to the person you need to be in human community—that is, your genuine self. Thus when you live by this ethic, you do not strive constantly to meet others' unrealistic standards and then berate yourself when you don't measure up. Rather, as one contributor to the larger human picture, you set reasonable expectations for yourself, and if your efforts prove ineffective, you pull back and simply try another approach. Through experience, this ethic reveals the paradox that if you try to *please* everyone you enslave yourself. But if you try to *serve* everyone, including yourself, you actually liberate yourself.

Commitment to the common good is the ethic for which you were born and through which you can fully express your social nature. It joins with the psychology of interdependence to give you both the direction and social security you need to let go of your perfectionism and cultivate the freedom you've always sought.

There is one more requisite commitment:

3. THE LAW OF LOVE

Love is the dominant, primal energy of life. It was here before we arrived, and its presence brought us into being. Because it is the defining principle of our humanity, we become whole to the degree that we are able and willing to receive and give love. Thus we must love in order to live and live in order to love. Someone put it this way: Love is the transcendent value that makes all other worthwhile values possible. Indeed, it is love that enables us to rise above our insecurities and be both comfortable with ourselves and at home in the universe.

At its primary, most elemental level, **love is** *acceptance.* Those who love you take you just as you are. Then they expect you to view yourself **as already accepted by them,** in spite of your limitations, your failures, and all that you find unacceptable in yourself. They know you are not perfect and need to grow beyond who you are at the moment, but the fact that you are imperfect does not deter them from accepting you. **Love offers you** *unconditional acceptance.*

From one side of the coin love, we receive favor that is not deserved. If you have car trouble along the road and a stranger stops to assist you and refuses to accept payment for it, that's a work of love. If co-workers accept you at your new job without requiring you to prove yourself worthy of them, they've done a loving thing.

On the flip side of the coin, love withholds judgment that *is* deserved. So if people love you, they don't reject you because you're imperfect, or make mistakes or act unacceptably. They also don't automatically require restitution when you disappoint them or take revenge against you if you violate them.

This unconditional love is perfect because:

- It can't be criticized or improved upon—you can't imagine anything better.
- It receives us perfectly—it freely accepts us *just as we are*.
- It values us enough to ask for our best.
- It perfectly bonds us to others—it leaves nothing between us and them.
- It creates hope, peace, and joy, the bases of perfect human experience.
- It insists, by its very nature, on social justice, the perfect human ethic.

The perfection of love makes it rise above everything else of worth in this world. And apropos of our concern here: **The perfection of love's acceptance can liberate us from the struggle of trying to be perfect all the time.** In combination with psychological interdependence and service to the common good, it gives us insight into our nature as social beings and offers us the perfect foundation, resource, and guide in our quest for personal wholeness.

To ignore this law is to pay a terrible price. To live by it is to find the joy we've always been looking for.

THE LIMITS OF CONDITIONAL ACCEPTANCE

As we have seen, the central issue of perfectionism is our deeply felt need for acceptance. As we were being raised to be nice people, we unconsciously and unconditionally bought the propositions that (1) conditional acceptance is the law of life, and (2) we must do the best we can with it. We agreed to jump through endless social hoops and in a sense, as someone has said, pay for everything. So we strive to be perfect all the time, occupied incessantly with symbols of accomplishment and signs of acceptance: a smile, a pat on the back, a positive comment, a kiss, a round of applause, a written commendation, a bonus, and, finally, perhaps, that legendary gold watch when we retire.

Conditional acceptance traditionally expresses itself in three forms: (1) *possible* acceptance—others may accept you, or they may not; (2) *partial* acceptance—they will accept parts of you, but not others; and (3) *temporary* acceptance—they will accept you for a period of time, but not forever. In any form, people who accept you conditionally have calculated your worth to them. No matter what they tell you about their friendship, they mean things like:

> I'll accept you *as long as* you meet my standards.
> I'll put up with you *until* I have reason not to like you.
> On *the condition* you continue to please me, I'll continue to accept you.

We must acknowledge that conditional acceptance and social expectations have their place. Achievement determines our success in education, the arts, athletics, politics, and, of course, the world of work: You won't sell art that people are unwilling to pay for; you're only as good as your last game; and if you don't produce at work, someone may fire you. Conditional contracts based on expected performance and backed by the threat of rejection play a major role in motivating us in this competitive world.

But conditional acceptance has assumed a place and role in our lives that it doesn't deserve. It can drive us to high levels of performance, but it forever denies us the assured acceptance we crave so deeply. Thus—and it's critical for you to see this—conditional acceptance is not worthy to define who you are, direct your life, determine how you feel about yourself, or tell you how to approach your valued relationships. Yes, you can want to feel good about how you perform and have others admire what you produce. But you cannot count on conditional acceptance to fulfill your life or provide you with inner peace and joy.

So what's the alternative?

UNCONDITIONAL LOVE

Love asks us to stop trying to please everyone all the time in order to win their acceptance, and simply accept the fact we're already accepted. In other words, it encourages us to *accept* **our acceptance**, which is, ultimately, to accept ourselves. As perfectionists, no matter how nicely we behave, we're anxious about whether we're acceptable to the universe. We say to ourselves,

If people only knew what I'm *really* like . . . We assume they would invalidate and reject us. But love says we're both valid and accepted no matter what we're like. With love, no one is counted out. And the decision to live day in and day out as **if we are already accepted** replaces our insecurity and striving with a contentment no one can take from us.

Human life operates in such a way that when we are convinced we are accepted as we are and are able and willing to accept ourselves and others in the same way, we not only put ourselves at peace, but we also transform both our inner character and our relationships so that we become more fully ourselves. It is trust in unconditional love that enables us to become functional adults and develop rewarding relationships.

When you realize for the first time that you are loved and you accept your acceptance, you know you are at one with what life is all about. Unconditional acceptance gives you the grounding and freedom and joy you need in order to be whole. So when you respond to love this way, you no longer need to be mired in perfectionism and in relationships that are less than liberating and satisfying.

But how do you accept your acceptance?

ACCEPTING YOUR ACCEPTANCE

To begin, you choose to look at life through the lens of love. In other words, you decide to see acceptance— rather than punitive judgment and rejection—at the beginning, middle, and end of your life. Have you ever seen the joyful tears of a mother and father as they cradle their newborn for the first time? To accept your acceptance begins with seeing that the love that drives the universe holds you in the same way and will never let you go.

To focus this lens, you draw on your own observations and common sense and make a choice. In other words, you trust that you are already accepted just like you decide to live as if the earth is round rather than flat; you count on evidence from your own experience that you cannot deny. In the same way that you trust astronomers, globe makers, and world travelers about our planet, you place your confidence in your own experience and in the consistent testimony of the most respected, profound voices of history who speak to your deepest personal needs. They all tell you that love is what makes life work right. They claim that nothing can nourish, ennoble, liberate, enlarge your spirit, and help to make you whole as much as your personal acceptance and practice of an accepting unconditional love. And once this notion that you are already accepted clicks inside you and you say, "Aha! I get it!" the decision to live in light of such accepting love may be as easy as opening your arms to a lover's passionate embrace.

Having said this, experience tells us that the simple choice to accept the fact that you already are accepted is not always easy. Deep in your heart, you may yearn for the assurance of acceptance that love promises. You may agree there is nothing you need more than to know you are loved, to accept that love, and then to love yourself and others. And both your stressful striving to please others and your ongoing sense of estrangement from everything may be feeling intolerable. But, in fact, at the very same time, strangely, you also may be resisting the choice to accept your acceptance. If this is the case—no matter the reason—your ability to make this choice will depend on the courage and willingness to choose, as well as on a knowledge of love.

So what might overcome your resistance, give you the courage to accept yourself, and free you to put your perfectionism behind you?

UNDESERVED FORGIVENESS

Someone could extend an extravagant favor to you that you feel you do not deserve. Perhaps a person you violate forgives, kisses, and embraces you. The stark beauty of such an act might shake you free to accept not only that forgiveness, but also the deeper and broader forgiveness of which it is merely an immediate expression.

ACCEPTANCE BY OTHERS

People you admire and who make sense to you could tell you they accept you as you are. They might say they're glad you are in their lives even though you often disappoint them. Such words may not be as powerful as a passionate kiss and embrace, but they can be liberating nevertheless.

A SENSE OF DESPERATION

You could come to the end of your rope with conditional acceptance. Sick of trying to prove yourself, with no sense of ever being good enough, you might, in sheer desperation, with nothing to lose, stare into the unknown and, rising above your resistance to accept yourself, take what people call a blind leap of faith.

Any one of these experiences might generate the courage you need to accept yourself. But what if no one ever lavishes love on you? Or what if you are dissatisfied with your perfectionism but not desperate? Suppose you're still resistant to change? What might free you to accept your acceptance?

A PERSONAL EXPERIMENT

In this case, you *do* something, rather than let something happen to you. What you do would develop something like this: You would contract with yourself for two, or, even better, three months, to practice accepting everyone you know and everyone you meet. In other words, you would not require people to pass any sort of test before you're willing to associate with them. You would practice unconditional love.

A primary purpose of the experiment would be to see if unconditional acceptance will liberate others from trying to please you all the time and thereby bring authenticity to your relationships. In the end, you would be trying to discern the difference between the effects of conditional and unconditional acceptance in order to decide, when the experiment is finished, which one you'll give priority to in your everyday life.

Of course, you would relate to people in ways that suit the particular relationship you want with them. In other words, the experiment doesn't ask you to initiate instant intimacy with everyone who comes across your path. For example, the depth and breadth of the acceptance you would offer to a new person at work would be different from the love you extend to your spouse. So while you would make yourself open to everyone, you would give off signals to help each of them understand the nature of the relationship you want.

It's also important to note that you would not immediately be accepting people to please them or get them to like you: That's the old trap of trying to be perfect. So you would not let anyone walk on you. Yes, you would make yourself vulnerable to betrayal by assuming people's goodwill and being open to their weaknesses as well as their strengths. But to accept them unconditionally is not an invitation for them to take advantage of you. Thus, were someone to become abusive, you would put a stop to it immediately, including refusing to be in their company until they could show respect for you. And of course, if they sincerely apologized, you would forgive them, freeing both them and you from judgment and rejection. But you contribute to others' problems by letting them exploit your love. True lovers neither reject other people out of hand nor allow others to walk all over them. They care about others *and* themselves.

To increase the chances of this experiment's success, you might let people know how you will be treating them and why. Telling them will not only enable them to understand what is going on; it will help seal your commitment to the experiment. It also might enlist their support of your effort to transform yourself into someone who enjoys accepting imperfect people and who is coming to see that you no longer have to be perfect yourself.

If the experiment fails—that is, if love's acceptance proves no more enriching than conditional acceptance—

then you can go back to embracing only those who never disappoint you. And you can return to your own burdensome struggle to please everybody all the time. At least you will know you have given love a fair chance.

Of course, I'm putting all my chips on unconditional acceptance. I'm betting you'll experience the irresistible paradox everyone finds who tries it: **Do something for people they don't deserve and withhold judgment they do deserve, and you enrich yourself. In other words, love them as they are for** *their benefit,* **and the one who gets the most out of it is you.**

Another side benefit of this experiment is that your acceptance can enable people to be positive and loving toward themselves and others, including, and especially, you. Not everyone will be immediately changed. But love always has been contagious. In a mysterious yet predictable fashion, it reproduces itself, radically transforming people, bringing out the best in them and moving them toward healthy relationships and wholeness.

I remember two of my junior high teachers. My friends and I used to talk about them all the time. As the school year began, one immediately tried to impress us with how tough she was, how important her subjects and standards were, and how unimportant were most of the things we were interested in. Right away we felt her disrespect and the rejection she threatened if we didn't prove ourselves to her. She was known not only for being unhappy and disliked, but also for failing to get students to perform well in class. In contrast, the other teacher was affirming. She trusted us, listened to our comments, talked with us about things we were interested in, treated us as individual persons. Not surprisingly, she was known for getting the best out of her pupils. Everyone who knew her said, "**She loves her students.**"

The practice of love, along with commitments to interdependence and the common good, will bring you joy, the highest human elation. Knowing you are loved generates joy in you. Your joy becomes unspeakably full when you, in turn, love others by serving their deepest need for acceptance. Expressing love gives birth to the inner richness you've always sought but never found in your endless efforts as a people-pleaser.

Making the commitment to accept yourself and others just as you are can free you to drop your perfectionism and begin this satisfying way to live. Of all the people I've met, those who have made this choice are the most liberated and joyful. In addition, the healthiest among them have learned to handle their imperfections in ways that expand their freedom and joy.

HANDLING YOUR IMPERFECTIONS

Assume that you've chosen to accept your acceptance, but you still find that living in this world with your flaws and failures is difficult (in other words, like most of us, you have not fully accepted yourself). To experience the freedom and joy I'm talking about, it's important to come to terms with the fact that you still have shortcomings and acknowledge them openly. It's neither necessary nor helpful to be ashamed of being human and to live every day trying desperately to cover your imperfections.

Someone has said, The good thing about being obviously imperfect is that you bring so much joy to others. It's another paradox: Let it be seen that you're imperfect and you make people happy; try to be perfect all the time and you turn off the very ones you're trying to impress. So the idea is to aim for excellence when the results promise appropriate satisfaction, as long as you keep in mind you are not and do not need to be perfect.

Here are some ways to reinforce your acceptance of your imperfection.

PRACTICE THINKING BEFORE YOU MAKE COMMITMENTS

Don't take on anything of any consequence on automatic pilot. Stop yourself before you act and ask, What will happen if I don't do this perfectly? and, How much time and energy is this commitment worth?

TALK TO YOURSELF ABOUT YOUR UNPRODUCTIVE EFFORTS AT EXCELLENCE

When you're taking far too long to perfect something, you can say to yourself, I've worked on this for hours and it doesn't deserve twenty minutes, or ask, Why am I spending so much time on this? What's the worst thing that can happen if I don't do this perfectly? How can I wrap this up and live with it? If you stop what you are doing and *talk tough* to yourself, it will help you take charge of your time. (I wish I had done this back in the seventies when I spent long hours reworking notes to friends because I was afraid that smudges or bad grammar would hurt me.)

STOP TAKING YOURSELF TOO SERIOUSLY AND JUDGING YOURSELF TOO HARSHLY

We all tend to overestimate the interest of others in judging our performances. Have you noticed that when you fret and work hard to impress them, they usually don't notice? In fact, they're too busy thinking about themselves, concerned about how they're coming across to **you** and what **you're** thinking of them. And think about it: When **they** make mistakes, it's no big deal; you sympathize with them and you don't write them off. Actually, you are much easier on them than you are on yourself. The idea is to accept the fact that you're a mistake-maker; you're going to blow it from time to time just like everyone else. When you don't live up to others' expectations, life is not going to fall apart. And when you make a mistake, unless you've seriously violated someone or committed a crime, more than likely it's not going to matter one bit tomorrow.

AGREE WITH PEOPLE WHO RIGHTLY CRITICIZE YOU

Criticism pains us because it pierces and cracks the image of perfection we work so hard to construct for ourselves and others. When you've met your deepest need to be loved, you can let go of that image and live with the **perfectly accepted imperfect you.** So if a neighbor criticizes you for driving forty in a twenty-five-mile-per-hour zone on your street, you can say, "You're right, I was driving too fast." If you had a reason for speeding you're not ashamed of, offer it: "I was rushing my friend to the hospital!" But when you're criticized, and you deserve it, it's liberating to state your agreement as a matter of fact and not defend yourself.

CRITIC: You stay up late again and you'll be exhausted tomorrow.
YOU: That's true, I will.

CRITIC: You look sloppy. You don't care about your appearance.
YOU: I think you are right; neatness is not one of my strengths.

CRITIC: That was a stupid thing to do.
YOU: Absolutely. It was not smart at all.

CRITIC: You never should have said that.
YOU: I know. From time to time I say the wrong thing.

CRITIC: You're either being sarcastic or agreeable.
YOU: I'm being agreeable.

You don't need to be perfect anymore. You now can deflect the power of criticism and benefit from it, something you've been unable to do before.

AVOID PEOPLE WHO ALWAYS EXPECT YOU TO PLEASE THEM

At any time, you may have those in your life who constantly criticize you for not being perfect. If they insist on their expectations, you may need to break these relationships. In their place, you can cultivate friendships with those who bring out the best in you, those people who expect your best but do not require you to be the best at everything you do.

Fortunately, teachers, bosses, spouses, and others who mean a lot to you usually expect you to perform to levels suited to your relationships rather than to be superhuman. They will want you to do your best, perform to your potential, and meet realistic expectations. If ever, however, you are trying to do your best and they don't realize it or judge you unfairly, you do not need to let them get away with it; you'll have enough trouble breaking the perfectionism habit without having them push you back into it. You can explain your need for people who do not expect you to be perfect. Most people will listen to reason when you're direct with them. If they are important to you and continue to press their unrealistic expectations, you can ask them to join you in getting a third party to mediate your dispute.

PRACTICE THE FOLLOWING THREE *PERFECT* WAYS TO RELATE TO OTHERS

1. **Do what suits each of your relationships.** Treat your spouse, children, boss, associates, friends, and acquaintances appropriately. (If your boss gives you a fitting, reasonable assignment, do it.) When you fulfill the appropriate expectations of your relationships, you're acting *perfectly*.

2. **Whenever you fail, apologize and, when fitting, offer restitution.** If in a lapse of memory you leave

friends stranded, you can offer apologies. Look them straight in the eye and tell them you were irresponsible and regret what you did. If you do something that takes money out of others' pockets, apologize and repay it. When these people accept your apologies and restitution, you've taken away the barriers between you and them and completely (that's *perfectly*) restored your relationships. (If you fail to apologize at the appropriate time, and realize it later, you then can apologize for what you did and for not acknowledging it earlier.)

3. If your apologies are rejected, tell them that you want things to be right between you, and that you feel powerless in the face of their rejection. Let them know you care. Tell them you value them and don't know what else to do. You may not redeem the relationships in question, but you've done all you can (that's *perfect*), you've made yourself completely (that's *perfectly*) vulnerable, and you've totally (that's *perfectly*) accepted the fact you live in an imperfect world.

Do I return you to a debilitating perfectionism with these *perfect* ways? No. Just the opposite. These behaviors are readily doable, they don't load you with the self-destructive pressures of perfectionism, and, with the acceptance of your imperfections, they counter any tendency you have to return to trying always to perform perfectly.

YOU'VE ADOPTED A NEW WAY TO LIVE

You now know you cannot always please others and, perhaps, you've decided you'll no longer try. If you have also accepted your acceptance you will be dealing more realistically with your imperfections. From now on you will

- Weigh commitments before making them.
- Talk tough to yourself when you're trying to be perfect.
- Refuse to take yourself too seriously or be too hard on yourself.
- Agree with those who rightly criticize you.
- Avoid those who insist on your being perfect.
- Practice the three ways to relate perfectly to others.

Your perfectionist tendencies may haunt you but they no longer need control or depress you. You can retain your own realistic, high standards, but instead of always wondering, Am I pleasing everybody? you now can ask, Am I feeling more true to myself as a person? You'll still want others to like you. And it will continue to feel good when you meet the reasonable expectations of others who are important to you. And, yes, at times you'll give good energy to pleasing them. But you now can operate with a new tolerance for your imperfection and no longer suffer the burden of feeling unacceptable and unaccepted.

And you'll still be a *nice person*.

Mistake #2

TAKING ON TOO MUCH

Early in the week you spent your evenings doing your taxes, writing overdue personal letters, and working with friends on a walkathon. When Thursday night came, for the first time in weeks you had a couple of hours to dig into the novel you'd been dying to read. But when a friend called to ask for help with another community project, there was no question what you would say: "Of course, I'll be right over." And later that night you crawled into bed exhausted and angry.

One evening at our home in Oakland, in the early seventies, I stepped outside to whistle for Raider, our little black and silver terrier. But when I pursed my lips, nothing happened. I tried several times but to no avail, and I noticed that my chin and lips felt numb. I'd always been a great whistler, so my surprise quickly turned to concern. A few days later in my doctor's office I took a dozen tests and answered a hundred questions with no sign of any physical problem. Finally, he turned to me and asked, "How many hours per week do you work on the average?" I told him I didn't know, but it was probably too many. He then asked me to take the next three weeks to chart those hours and scheduled me for another appointment. As we sat down in his office for that second visit, I handed him a slip of paper that said *68 hours per week*.

He said, "Your inability to whistle is an early warning signal from your nervous system that you're not running your life correctly."

I learned that day that while we generally are healthier when we're doing what we enjoy, our bodies are not impressed by overwork no matter how good our intentions or noble our commitments. That night, by phone, I resigned from two committees, cut a couple of low priorities out of my daily routine, and immediately scaled down my workweek to 50 to 53 hours. That load proved to be reasonable for me in my midthirties with a two-minute commute. And as you might guess, the whistle soon came back.

Whether we're aware of it or not, when we take on too much for an extended period of time we damage ourselves. Sooner or later stress makes us scattered, forgetful, and susceptible to sleep disorders. We become the jugglers who put too many balls in the air, who burn candles at both ends, who sail overloaded ships that are listing and sinking.

And usually, without our being conscious of it, our niceness traps us: If we say no to someone's request for our time, we feel selfish and guilty; if we try to do everything asked of us, a relentless tiredness saps our vitality, our effectiveness, and our enjoyment of life.

Mistake #2: Taking on Too Much

When we take on too much we also become angry deep down, although, as with our entrapment, we don't think about it. Sadly, we not only direct this anger at those who ask things of us—which is unfair—but also at ourselves for saying yes. And the anger we turn inward inevitably leads to depression.

The popular term for this post-modern, debilitating condition is *burnout.*

As living organisms in a complex, fast-lane society, we expend energy every day in activities that add pleasure and excitement to our lives. But they also drain our energy and submit us to constant tension. To relieve this stress and replenish our vitality, we eat, sleep, exercise, relax, take breaks, change our pace, engage in various forms of recreation, and, perhaps, use alcohol, nicotine, caffeine, or other drugs. But whenever we overdose on activities that deplete us without restoring what we've spent, we feel empty and dry, and our unrelieved stress turns into distress. And in the same way as when we try to be perfect, we end up neither living well nor enjoying ourselves.

As a nice person, you've always known that to take on too much is self-defeating. But you've also believed it's what you're supposed to do. And even if you've wanted to stop, you haven't known how, or you've unconsciously assumed you can't. Accordingly, you remain in danger of burnout for the rest of your life. It may not be of much comfort, but if you often are captive to the stress, depression, and exhaustion that goes with taking on too much, you are not alone. Fortunately, you can do something about it. First, you need to understand why you engage in it.

OUR PURPOSE IN TAKING ON TOO MUCH

Some of us find we have too much to do today just to survive in our fast-moving world. But when asked why we overextend ourselves, we nice people say that more than survival is involved: We live for something larger than ourselves. We want to help our friends or improve our communities. We want to contribute to the common good. At a conscious level these are noble purposes and our intentions are well meaning. But, as I found out, even the best of intentions do not protect us from burnout. And whenever we overload our lives, much more is usually going on than immediately meets the eye.

Whenever we try to be perfect, behind any noble purposes we have lies our desperate need to be accepted. It is this same unexpressed need that most often drives us to take on too much. In **trying to be perfect** we worked on the *quality* of our activities: Was that good or clever enough? Did I impress them with how well I did that? In **taking on too much,** we stress the *quantity* of what we do: Have I done enough? Perhaps if I do just **one more thing** they will be compelled to like me.

Of course, this endless striving is unnecessary because we're already accepted by the love that defines what it means to be human. The task is to accept our acceptance and live in the freedom love lavishes on us. So if you've already done this, you've taking a major step to alleviate the social pressures to be perfect and to take on too much.

THE REASON WE TAKE ON TOO MUCH

I spent the early years of my professional life trying to enhance my reputation as a nice and competent person. I sincerely wanted to perform well and usually was effective at what I did. But, without my realizing it, my interest in impressing others often competed with serving them. When teaching, I often was more interested in compliments from members of my classes than I was in the satisfaction of the teaching experience itself. And to keep the positive feedback coming, I went beyond reasonable limits for myself, wasted both time and energy, exhausted myself, and often did less of a job than I was capable of doing. On the day the doctor traced my inability to whistle to my taking on too much, I learned not only that this was harmful, but also that I was unaware of why I did it and what I hoped to gain by it. And this discovery drove me to probe further why I—and other nice people—insisted on making this mistake.

At rock bottom, I found that both mistakes—trying to be perfect and taking on too much—are based on two popular miscalculations. The first is that conditional acceptance is the law of life, and the second says that no one has reason to value us just as we are. Both of these assumptions lead us to self-doubt and low self-worth. And I, along with other nice people, obviously, unconsciously to some degree, had bought into both of them.

The seeds of self-doubt and low self-worth usually are sown in our earliest years. Alongside our parents and other adults, we were small, inexperienced, and weak, without much knowledge and unsure of ourselves. While they may have tried to make us feel special at times, they often gave us signals that our opinions, feelings, and needs were not important. They may have made it clear that we were not to speak unless spoken to, and that they expected us to take what we were given and do what we were told. At times, they may have made us feel we were in the way.

In our innocence as children, we chose to agree with their assessment of our place and importance in society. The secret things we did for which we felt ashamed—things we carefully kept from everyone else—loomed large in our own eyes. Our appearance and physical limitations also made it hard for us to esteem ourselves appropriately; most of us, at least at times, felt dreadfully bony, pudgy, gawky, clumsy, or even ugly. Thus we gave ourselves low grades in worth. Insecure as we were, and especially as we entered the turmoil of the teenage years, we reinforced these low self-ratings by dwelling on our failures and less attractive features, and by comparing our weaknesses with the strengths of our peers.

Because of my birth date, I was always the youngest boy in my school classes. Early on, my favorite subjects were recess, lunch, and gym, which didn't impress my teachers. In contrast, the more mature girls acted as if they enjoyed doing homework, and they consistently earned good grades. I settled for C's in most subjects, not just because I played more than I studied, but because I had come to feel stupid compared to them and was terrified of competing and of risking further embarrassment. And as I tried to prove myself on the playground, every report card reinforced my image of myself as a mediocre student. It was not until my junior year in college that I saw that I was living down to a negative picture of myself and my past record, rather than living up to my capabilities. Fortunately, about that time I also realized I owed more to myself and the world than I was offering, and I began to apply myself. I think I was afraid of being left behind.

With most of us who were raised to be nice, our negative self-images grew up with us and we grew into them, allowing them to define who we think we are and letting them become self-fulfilling prophecies that continue to dictate how we run our lives. When we see the power of such self-judgment, we can begin to understand why we take on too much: If we feel inferior, unimportant, or unworthy, we kill ourselves trying to prove we aren't—we not only say yes to every request of those whose approval we crave, but, in spite of already being busy, we may offer to do things for them before they ask.

TRANSFORMING YOUR LOW SELF-WORTH

If you've accepted your acceptance, you've done so based on a view of reality that affirms your value. It makes sense to reason, If I were not worth anything, the love that holds at the center of the universe would not count me worthy of acceptance. And if you have known the unconditional love of family or friends, it can serve as a mirror in which you can perceive your true self. This perspective has given you, therefore, a boost, or a head start in transforming your poor sense of self-worth.

The problem is that you may continue out of habit,

as I did, to carry with you the self-image you adopted in childhood. As we saw earlier, the child we once were remains within us and is very much a part of our present selves. The psychologists tell us we must understand, accept, and integrate this child if we want to be free from the child's unmet needs and be healthy adults. An early step in constructing a positive self-image is to note that although we understand why we downgraded our worth when we were children, it is neither appropriate nor necessary to do it as adults.

Historically, adults have used three building blocks to construct a positive self-image.

1. Success based on society's standards. This view contends that if you get good grades in school, have smashing good looks, star on a team, win awards, or become rich and powerful, you have worth. Worth based on success is one of the most powerful driving forces in our society. But like conditional acceptance, to which it's related, success according to these definitions has several problems: It's not readily accessible to less gifted, weak, or poor people; it can come and go at any time, lasting only as long as you meet the standards of others; it makes you prove yourself all the time, both to others and yourself; and it compels you to compete constantly with others, always to do better and, too often, to do too much.

2. Service to the common good. Here is the idea that you have worth when you contribute to the world's needs for shelter, clothing, peace, wisdom, justice, knowledge, health services, beauty, communication, hope, environmental renewal, business, transportation, freedom, and love—anything that sustains the integrity and health of the community of life and makes living worthwhile. As an ethic, it guides and empowers us to fulfill our purpose as interdependent, social animals. It also is justly accessible to everyone and, from the standpoint of what enriches us deep down inside, it's a quantum leap beyond simply living to gain wealth and power for our own benefit.

This second building block, however, like the first one, depends on performance. Thus the satisfaction it offers—just like the satisfaction that comes with social success—can seduce us into taking on too much. It makes us think we're worthy only when we are too busy, when we outdo ourselves, when we sacrifice for others or, in the extreme, when we are actually suffering. So while it is essential that we commit ourselves to serving the common good rather than focusing simply on our own social or material success, we need to remind ourselves that we can burn out on noble as well as selfish causes.

3. Appreciation of your worth as a human being. This notion insists that as a member of the human species you are important, just the way you are, with no qualifications, no matter what anyone says. It sees you as a dynamic center of creative possibility: You are able to absorb knowledge, develop skills, and effect changes for the better; you have the capacity to make life richer for others and yourself, bringing out the best in everyone you touch. This particular perspective affirms your worth by contending that **no one else can do the constructive things you can do in your particular time and place, with your unique gifts.** Thus, it counters the negative self-image you developed as a child and still may be tolerating as an adult. And because you are of great worth, it says you deserve to use your energy and time in responsible ways of your own choosing, rather than take on too much.

It is true that we seldom live up to our own potential or meet either the expectations we set for ourselves or the standards by which we judge others. No matter how well-meaning we are, ignorance, misunderstanding, prejudice, peer pressure, and emotional immaturity often keep us from doing our best. And history shows that under these powers and certain menacing circumstances—which we hope we never have to face—we nice people are capable of mischief, malicious spirit, violence, and barbaric evil. Yet, in spite of our dark sides, our shortcomings and uncountable contradictions, you and I are mysterious and marvelous creatures who are worthy of respect, beginning with respect from ourselves. And when we allow the fact that we are loved to eradicate our low sense of self-worth, we are capable of creating relationships and communities of love.

Of course, you deserve esteem not just for your potential, but also for what you're actually doing with your life. You've learned that it is important to **accept yourself just the way you are, but not** *stay* **just the way you are.** You've seen the disparity between your *actual self* (who you are this very moment) and your *true self* (who you can be at your grounded, liberated, integrated, balanced best), and you're working to bridge that gap. You're giving serious energy to developing your physical, intellectual, psychological, emotional, social, moral, ethical, and spiritual sides, to becoming more effective, mature, and happy. Right now you're reading this book to improve your self-knowledge and skills.

The point of this third building block is that you matter and are worthy of respect, even if you aren't rich and famous. Whatever use you make of the first two blocks, it's important to adopt a positive picture of yourself simply on the basis of who you are and what you have to offer. **You may not be as strong and competent as you wish you were, but neither are you as weak or inept as you think you are.** Such a balanced assessment may not immediately erase the low self-image you've allowed to limit your sense of worth, but it will enable you to see how distorted that image is and begin to replace it. It will give you the foundation to build both the character and confidence you need to account for yourself and cope creatively with adversities. You also can begin to form healthier relationships, because you can respect not only others but yourself, and because you will not need to place yourself in subordination to them.

The point is that to see yourself this way can free you to be imperfect and to avoid taking on too much. Indeed, you will not have to say yes automatically in order to be **special, because you'll know you already are.** It also can liberate you to say to someone close to you: "For the first time in my life, I'm going to appreciate who I am. I now see that to do well by you, I must take care of my own needs and conserve my own time and energy by not taking on too much."

But suppose your sense of self-worth is so low and so deep-seated that you're not able—at least on the first try—to make these positive self-affirmations. You have plenty of company and need not despair. You can work on it. Here are three exercises to do:

1. Praise Your Strengths

Instead of looking at your weaknesses, shortcomings, and failures today, concentrate on—and list in a column—your good points: your wit, organizing ability, love of nature, artistic or musical talent, social concern, poetic or scientific mind, way with children, productiveness, cheerful nature, patience, commitment to fairness, thoughtfulness, good memory, consideration for others, whatever. If you have trouble writing genuinely good things about yourself, identify strengths that loved ones say they see in you. Read your list over and over to yourself. Review it each day for a month. When you strengthen your awareness of your good points, you can see yourself as one who has both the right and the responsibility to say no when appropriate.

2. Say No through Visualization

Think of busy people you respect. In your mind, put yourself in their place, politely saying no to a specific request for their time. Imagine a similar situation in which you soon may find yourself. Listen to yourself say no. Run the scene through several times in your imagination. Say, "No. No. No. No!" Enjoy how great it feels to say it. Impress yourself, also, with the fact that you have fantasized the avoidance of saying a yes that you later on would have resented and regretted. Try these imaginings for a week. Or, for a change, visualize various situations relevant to your own experience and watch yourself say no in each one. And then enjoy reveling in your growing self-respect.

3. Say No in Real-Life Situations

The next time someone asks you to do something that makes you feel the least bit uncomfortable or creates the slightest hesitation in you, say, **"I'm sorry, I'm going to say no."** Approach each social encounter consciously as a person who doesn't have to say yes to every request. Say no because you already have enough on your plate. Say no to establish a healthier habit pattern—one firm refusal will help you start to break the old habit of saying yes. Say no for the sheer fun of it—you've been overloaded and not having much fun lately.

To hold a high view of yourself, you do not have to denigrate others, put yourself first all the time, or say no automatically when people want something from you. You simply have to take appropriate care of yourself, which means saying no whenever you are already committed to more important matters. Both your intimate and businesslike relationships demand much from you, and your time and energy resources are limited. So when you think well of yourself, it is important to weigh your various commitments and thoughtfully negotiate, with yourself and others, any new undertakings.

If you trust yourself to the universe by accepting your acceptance and build on the idea that you have worth just because you're human, you have a running start at establishing a strong sense of self. In turn, you can nurture this sense by living as if you have worth and by making your life more effective. You can do the latter by setting worthy goals, by making specific plans to reach them, and by designing a thoughtful balance for your life.

ORCHESTRATING A BALANCED LIFE

If you've accepted yourself and raised your sense of self-worth by a sound appreciation of who you are, you should find it less difficult than in the past to balance your life by managing your time. At the same time, it still may not be easy. This especially will be true if you haven't the slightest idea of what to do, or if you always have thought—and continue to think—that all you need to run your life are good intentions and spontaneity. Many people believe that if you're nice, your life will automatically fall in line. So, in part, you may be taking on too much and suffering burnout because you don't have a plan. If so, know that life-planning today is not a luxury or an extracurricular activity; it's a necessary survival skill. Yes, life is more than time management. But if you don't manage your life, you will not be able to attain the critical balance needed for negotiating your way through today's world.

Balance has two dimensions, both of which can be illustrated by the bicycle. To remain upright, you must steer between the pushes and pulls of life's polar opposites: too rational/too emotional; too much/too little; too fast/too slow; too traditional/too innovative; too cautious/too reckless; too serious/too silly; too big/too small; too hot/too cold; too strong/too weak—the list is endless. Balance requires you to retain a sizable portion of each side of these opposites, to live in between, to be a *both/and* person instead of one who's *either/or*, out of balance and always falling to one side or the other.

The second image you can use to understand balance is the juggler on a bike. Imagine pumping along, letting go of the handlebars, and keeping objects of various weights, sizes, and textures in the air. Let them represent your ongoing activities that consume different amounts of time and energy: brushing your teeth, commuting, eating, working, resting, gardening, reading, watching the six o'clock news, paying bills, making love, and so on.

Your task is to give these activities the attention, time, and energy they deserve, based on how much they're worth to you.

Life today is like riding a bike up and down roads that are bumpy, curvy, and hilly while juggling bananas, balloons, and bowling balls. No matter how you negotiate turns and potholes, like everyone else, you get out of balance at times, drop the ball—or banana—or fall on your face. Fortunately, when this happens, you can get up and start over by pedaling hard to regain equilibrium as soon as possible. But the main point is to manage your days, weeks, and months so you ride through life in basic balance.

So how do you achieve this?

First, you take care of your primary human needs, including family and friends, edifying play and work, creative expression, physical and spiritual nourishment, contribution to the common good, rest, exercise, information, wisdom, and planning. When you meet these basic needs, you give yourself a strong foundation for a balanced life.

Of course, you also must regularly take care of a number of routine tasks that are secondary but very important in today's world, such as banking, shopping for necessities, getting a haircut, maintaining your car, doing favors for others—another one of those lists that seem endless.

There are three keys to keeping these primary and secondary endeavors in rewarding balance: (1) develop long-range, worthwhile direction for your life, (2) make thoughtful responses to requests for your time and energy, and (3) manage your limited discretionary time effectively. The idea is to design your life as much as possible so you will not drift or spend all your time simply fending off what the world throws at you. If this is the way you want to live, there are three things you need to do.

1. DEVELOP LONG-RANGE, WORTHWHILE DIRECTION FOR YOUR LIFE

This means you start by deciding where you want to end up. A first step is to identify your greatest passion and make sure you give it the place in your life it deserves. Your passion is your first love. It is the source, the power, and the goal of your life. It starts your engine and keeps you on track to pursue your ultimate priorities.

Some of us are fortunate to express our passion through our work—we mesh **what we love to do** with **what we do to make a living.** Others of us must settle for work that is not entirely fulfilling, and then live to enrich and enjoy our families, or serve specific social causes, or simply try to make real differences in the world. But no matter where we channel our greatest passion, to the degree that it helps us contribute to the common good and make the world a better place, it gives us worthwhile purpose and direction for our lives.

Set Specific Goals

To maintain loyalty to this direction, however, we also must set specific, lifelong goals. I once heard someone state an important, self-evident truth: If you don't know where you're going, you may end up where you don't want to be and may not enjoy getting there. It suggests that aimlessness can cause you to drift and eventually miss your best possible life. A lack of long-range goals leaves you without focus, balance, or basic criteria to judge how best to live right now. It robs you of confidence in where you're going and thereby renders you tentative about what your priorities are at any given time. And this tentativeness makes you vulnerable to taking on too much.

Another basic axiom that we nice people tend to forget: No one ought to look back with regret. It reminds us that we have the responsibility and power to do what we need to do to experience wholeness, and it's incumbent upon us not to miss out on it. We owe it to ourselves not to betray our best interests. In other words, knowing you become what you are committed to, you must take care to ground yourself on solid values. Thus it will help to stop from time to time and ask, What are my real values? How am I expressing the best of them? What do I need and want to do with the rest of my life? Instead of the question, How much can I get done? we need to ask, Am I pursuing healthy and hopeful aspirations? Life is short and easily wasted. Answering these questions honestly helps you begin to come to terms with the reality of your mortality and come alive as you never have before.

To set goals that are compatible with the priorities to which your passion points, it's important to envision an appropriate, satisfying future for yourself. Your goals may be to have new experiences, achieve something special, or solve problems that presently beset you. No matter the case, the idea is to let your vision dictate your goals, keep you energized and on track, and enable you to monitor your progress. The more specific your vision and goals, the more clearly you'll be able to choose your priorities and avoid taking on too much.

It's true that the future is always an illusion—it's beyond our grasp and, in that sense, never real. Further, we don't have final control over how long we live, and we can't even be sure of tomorrow. This is one reason we're hearing so much about living in the now, taking life one day at a time, rather than counting on the future. But I'm not talking about living in the future, or even about your *real* future. I'm suggesting you envision for yourself a desirable enough future to provide you with hope right now. **By hope, I refer to the positive energy you experience when you possess a realistic and satisfying picture of what lies ahead.** It doesn't have to be a perfect picture; it simply must be good enough to get you up to face the day. The point is that your vision and goals will generate direction and energy for your life today, long before you reach them.

Plan Your Future

When you are ready to set goals for your life, you need a plan. As a framework for a plan, you can use figures from actuarial tables to determine how long you can expect to live barring unforeseen circumstances. In other words, begin by estimating your life span. Experts today put a woman's life span around eighty-five years, a man's at eighty. In figuring yours, consider your health, habits, disposition, attitudes, mental outlook, family history, support systems, financial picture, retirement prospects, climate and geography, and any other positive and negative factors that might affect your longevity. Women who register a positive in most of these areas may expect to live into their nineties. A healthy woman of forty, therefore, might calculate that she'll live another fifty years; a healthy man, forty to forty-five years. The point is to set your own reasonable figure.

Next, identify the important areas of your life: family, friends, income, work, housing, community service, recreation, education, travel, retirement, hobbies, etc. At the top of loose-leaf pages in a notebook or in a file set up in your word-processing program, print the names of each area, one to a page.

You can begin by setting your remaining life span figure (Is it sixty, thirty-five, fifteen years?) For sake of illustration, assume it's thirty-five. On each first page, under each area of designation, put the date and write *This Year.* On the next page in each area, write, *2–5 Years.* Beginning on page three start marking off a page each for years 5 to 10, 10 to 15, 15 to 20, 20 to 25, and, finally, perhaps, 25 to 35 years.

What you now have is a notebook whose pages essentially are empty but for the grids that cross the basic areas of your projected life with several time frames. Now, take a pencil and start with the pages that represent the last ten years of your life (twenty-five to thirty-five years from now, in this case), answering, What do I want to experience or accomplish in this area by the time my life is over? It's on these pages that you identify the larger, long-range goals for your life.

Once you've answered the question the best you can in all of the areas, start working backward in each area through the time frames, beginning with twenty to twenty-five years, now asking, What do I need to do *in this time frame* to make sure I attain what I ultimately want in this area?

In each area, move toward the present in incremental steps, calculating what you need to do in each time period to give you the best chance to accomplish your ultimate goals. You'll finally come to what you need to do in the next twelve months (*This Year*, page one) to attain what you want down the road. Then, as you range across your various goals, you can establish your highest priorities by numbering them on the basis of which you want to give the most attention, energy, time, and, perhaps, money.

To meet more costly goals, it will help to set up a savings schedule and pinpoint when you can pay for them. For example, suppose you think that in the area of travel you want to trek in the Himalayas, take the train to Canada's Lake Louise, browse the Louvre in Paris, escape to Maui or Miami every January, stand in awe before India's Taj Mahal (something I've dreamed of), and, perhaps, explore the geographical center of the Sahara (something I've never had the least interest in). List these trips in your twenty-five-to-thirty-five-year time frame for *Travel*, along with estimated costs. Weigh each one's value to you. If any are fanciful and out of sight financially, erase and forget them (too much fantasy will create the overload and regret you're trying to avoid).

Compare the costs of the remaining trips with your income and projected expenses in your other areas, eliminating any that don't compete. Then, in pencil, assign each trip to a particular time frame, and note in the preceding frames how much you'll need to save for it during those periods. If seeing the Taj Mahal is a high priority but the cost is daunting, you may have to put it off and save for many years. And if you can't save anything this year, identify the time frame when you can start, and then schedule it appropriately.

The key point: Once you commit to specific long-range goals, they will influence the way you live *right now.* Writing them down helps you see your goals, gives intentional direction to your life, and helps you avoid wasting time on low priorities. Of course, you can change your goals at any time. But having them established and clearly before you lets you assess current activities and eliminate those that fail to contribute to the future you envision.

Certainly you cannot control everything, but you can manage important facets of your life with worthwhile goals and reasonable schedules. And with this kind of long-range planning, you can begin to balance your life today and save yourself from aimlessness, overload, and burnout.

2. MAKE THOUGHTFUL RESPONSES TO REQUESTS FOR YOUR TIME AND ENERGY

You Do Not Have to Say Yes *Immediately*

You may be flattered and tempted by someone's request for help. You can avoid a damaging seduction by taking time to ascertain whether the task (1) contributes to the common good or your long-range priorities, (2) suits your skills, (3) can be done in spite of other commitments, and (4) will be enjoyable. Sometimes, of course, you might agree to do something you won't enjoy simply because it's important and has to be done, or because no one can do it but you, or because it is your turn, or because it comes as part of a larger commitment you've made. But normally you want to agree to do those things that meet this fourfold test.

If you are no longer automatically going to say yes to what others ask of you, it may help them to know what you're doing. You can say to them: "I am no longer going to burn myself out by doing everything people want of me. Please understand when I say no that I am trying to be realistic and responsible." Clarifying your new intentions may even garner their support.

Whenever anyone—a spouse, co-worker, or close friend—will be directly affected by a decision you'll make, it may help to confer with them beforehand. You do not want them to direct your life, but they're important to you. And while you may end up doing what you believe you need to do no matter what they say, if you consult with them before making your decision, they won't resent being ignored.

You Can Say No and Gain Respect for Yourself

When a request does not pass the fourfold test, to say no is to do everyone a favor. This means you can feel good about saying, "I'm sorry, but I'm going to say no." And you can pat yourself on the back because you just avoided taking on too much. And if you've never before said no, it may surprise you how good it feels.

When people ask you to do something, you ordinarily don't owe them an explanation when you say no. But you also don't have to be callous or uncaring. You might want to say, "Sorry, I'm not going to do that because . . ." And, if appropriate, you may want to add, "I'll let you know if I think of someone else you might ask."

When I'm asked to do something by colleagues that would be too taxing, I say something like, "I'm sorry, I'm going to say no. In the past, whenever I said yes to too much work, I ended up angry and didn't do a good job. I'm not doing that anymore." When I first said things like this, I repeatedly heard, "That's what I ought to do." And their respect and envy helped change how I felt about going to work.

My wife, Barbara, and I, like most couples, split various household tasks. I can remember saying to her a few years ago, "I know you want me to do that project Sunday, but with the Saturday we've planned, if I don't relax Sunday, I'll never face Monday. Please understand. I'll do it next Saturday." I knew I'd said the right thing, whether she would agree or not. When she said, "Okay, next Saturday's all right," it was icing on the cake.

Self-respect is basic to the wholeness we're all looking for. It may help to note that we respect people who say no when it's appropriate, and that we don't respect those who say yes when they shouldn't. In the same way, when people ask you to do something you ought not to do, and you say no, they'll respect you— even if they wanted you to say yes—simply because they see that you respect yourself. The idea is for you to say no when it would be harmful to say yes, and let the respect you gain from others and yourself enrich you.

You Can Avoid the Ripple Effect

Some roles and responsibilities lap over into others. Before you agree to chair the PTA, it helps to find out how much time it will take. You can't assume it means one monthly meeting. If you don't ask, and it requires you to confer with the principal twice a month, to meet with subcommittees and also attend regional conferences, you've allowed yourself to be a victim of the *ripple effect.* Whenever you're recruited to a task, it will help to get clarified what is required of you and say yes on those conditions alone. If requirements escalate, you always can renegotiate or resign.

If You Take on Something New, You Can Drop Something Else

But which commitment do you drop? Ask yourself, Which one gives me the least satisfaction? Which takes more from me than it returns? Which have I been carrying too long? Once you identify one (or more), drop it as soon as you can. Your choice may affect people important to you, so you will need to tell them. Be honest; blame it on your mental health.

In the same way, if an important activity suddenly requires more of you—and you want to continue it—drop something else. For a brief time you can over-schedule yourself without turning stress into distress. But you can't do it as a matter of course. Your well-being requires moderation, appropriateness, and balance based on being realistic about your limits.

3. MANAGE YOUR TIME EFFECTIVELY

Learning to balance your life takes discipline and time. A woman I knew who borrowed a book on time management from her local library apparently was short on both. When she finally returned the book, it was months overdue. It also hadn't been read.

The task is to manage better the time you must give to surviving and to use your discretionary time most effectively. No one else has the right or responsibility to do this for you—only you will deserve the credit and the blame for how you do it. Look at how you can do it well.

Each day contains just twenty-four hours. On average you'll probably spend ten of them on eating, sleeping, grooming, and personal hygiene. You'll give another ten or so, five days a week, to your work (including commuting, preparation, home study, and overtime). What do you have left? Part of the weekend and about four waking hours per day to squeeze in everything else—shopping, housework, auto maintenance, family, friends, community service, your finances, entertainment, other tasks and leisure activities.

This is a lot to cram into a few short hours. Thus, many people face life like a deer frozen in the headlights, or like a race car spinning its wheels on a slippery track. Your purpose is to manage your time, not letting it control you or get beyond your reach. Your goal is to accomplish what you can of your self-chosen priorities without trying to do it all—or have it all—and burning out. Even worthwhile and enjoyable tasks, if there are too many of them, can exhaust us and cause us to do everything we do poorly. Our time is limited, and we owe it to everyone not to burn out for either high priorities or low ones.

To manage your discretionary time will require a few basic choices and a few thoughtful minutes each day. Here are some ways to change yourself from simply a doer to an effective time manager.

Set Daily Priorities

Each night, you can jump-start the next day by making a list of things you think you will need to do. This will allow you to go to bed without the fear that you'll forget something important under the time pressures of the morning. And if you have a particular problem to solve the next day, making note of it will give your subconscious a chance to work on it while you sleep—many people who do this often wake in the morning with helpful solutions.

The point is to order first what is *most important*, instead of what is easiest, most fun, nearest at hand, or what only looks like a crisis. Number your tasks by their importance, taking deadlines and other time factors into consideration. Identify items to do during the morning #1, #2, #3, and perhaps #4, in a specific order. You can leave less immediate and important tasks, #5 through #12, for the afternoon or the next day.

Some people group their tasks for each day by assigning them a 1, 2, or 3 (or an a, b, or c) with the 1's being those most important or of highest priority based on deadlines. If you choose this plan, then you don't tackle any tasks numbered 2 until all the 1's are done, or any of the 3's until you've completed all the 2's. The day may end with none of the 2's and 3's accomplished. If it does, reassign them a new number for the next day, or drop them. If you find that you are dropping 3's that are too important, you're trying to do too much.

Work through your priorities by your own choice at your own pace. Doing a task quickly is often less important than doing it correctly. Save precious time by consolidating connected tasks: phone calls, trips to the mall, writing checks, etc. And perhaps most important is to choose the best task to do at a particular time.

You do not need to plan every minute of every day or spend your entire life organizing. But when you set priorities in these ways you'll feel less pressured, and you'll look back on each day feeling as though you've used your time the best you can.

Mistake #2: Taking on Too Much

Choose a Working Calendar that Suits Your Rhythm

To see a month on one page in your date book helps you plan ahead with a broader vision; a week to a page may free you to list your daily tasks just once, right on your calendar. Choose the one that gives you the most support and freedom.

Expect the Unexpected

Someone will surprise you with a call; your car will break down; your toilet will overflow; a meeting will go over time; a colleague will get sick; a customer will be late; you'll bump into an old friend. In today's world, delays, interruptions, and emergencies *are* your life. So leave holes in your days by blocking out a half hour here, an hour there. Mark them as *interruptions*. It will help you deal with the unexpected, control your life more effectively, take it in stride, and enjoy it more.

I taught a class for professional types on this subject, and two weeks later an attorney who had participated called me to say that he had started charting his daily calendar with four half-hour interruptions, and that he had never before experienced such control of his life.

Break Down Complex Tasks into Manageable Parts

You know it's not smart to try to eat a whole meal in one gulp. In the same way, you can cut a large project into bite-sized chunks. When you have to prepare your taxes, you may tend to put it off because the task seems overwhelming. And if you block out all day Saturday to do it, getting through the preceding week may be dreadful. So, instead, set aside one hour on Saturday to go through your checks. (Set a timer for an hour to stop you from getting bogged down.) Then block off another hour—perhaps on an evening the next week—to identify interest and taxes, another later on for business deductions, and another for contributions, and so on. Before you know it, you'll be finished.

Count on Tasks Taking Longer than Your Normal Estimates

Think of how often something has taken twice as long to do as you thought it would. We need to accept our own realistic pace to accomplish tasks—not some ideal one—and schedule more time than we think is necessary.

I counseled a mother who said yes to chairing the committee to plan her daughter's elementary school graduation. She figured it would take three evening meetings to do it, if everything went smoothly. And while she was anxious about the unknowns, she thought committee people might balk at four nights out. I asked her what would happen if she scheduled three meetings and it took four. She said, "I'll be stressed and the committee will be grouchy." She decided to ask them to block four evenings. They agreed, and they finished in three. She canceled the fourth and made everyone happy. And she learned that it's more enjoyable to achieve goals under realistic deadlines than stressful ones.

Delegate

As a nice person you want to be seen as caring and industrious, and you probably do a lot of tasks others can handle. But you do not need to take on everything within reach. As you set your schedule and begin your day, you can ask yourself, What can I turn over to someone else?

Schedule Ahead

You need breaks for rest, diversion, variety, refreshment, and times for slowing down, tasting life, doing what replenishes your energy. When you know that next month you'll need days to read, window-shop, watch videotapes, or do nothing at all, set aside blocks of time for them *now*, labeling in your date book exactly what they're for. Then, when people ask you to do something, you'll have a conflict: "I'm sorry, but I'm busy at that time."

Managing your time in these ways will help you balance your life, give you enjoyable days to which you can look forward, and make you less ready to take on too much.

LIVING WITH MORE VITALITY

You now realize that you have much to offer, and you do a lot of things well. You also have made a commitment no longer to overextend yourself and will enlist the support of family and friends to help you carry out your resolve. And you are going to set up long-range directions for your life. In addition, from now on, when asked for your time and energy, you will

- Stop to think before you say yes.
- Say no to tasks that do not suit you, tasks for which you do not have time or you do not enjoy.
- Say yes only when you have clarified what is expected of you.
- Drop a commitment whenever you take on a new one.

You'll also manage your time more effectively, because you will

- Set priorities each day for what you will do.
- Use a calendar that suits your schedule.
- Expect unexpected interruptions and plan accordingly.
- Break down complex tasks into manageable parts.
- Schedule more than enough time for each task.
- Delegate whatever you can to others.
- Mark off times for yourself, long in advance.

Look now at how our original scenario has changed:

You spent evenings early in the week doing your taxes, writing overdue personal letters, and working with friends on a walkathon. When Thursday night came, for the first time in weeks you had a couple of hours to dig into the novel you'd been dying to read. (You now schedule such times regularly.) So when a friend calls to ask for help with another community project, there now *is* a question about what you will do.

You'll answer it based on what your relationship is, how much time you've given him recently, and on how your life is balanced at the moment. You very well may say, **"I'm sorry, you've caught me at a busy time,"** and curl up with that book.

If you manage your life, you will avoid going to bed exhausted and angry and rising the next day depressed and burned out. Yes, it may happen—you are not perfect, remember? But you will not always try to be perfect and take on too much because you will not base your self-worth on whether you always please others or on how much you accomplish. Instead, you'll appreciate yourself and be in charge of your life, making decisions that enable you to make real contributions to the common good and, thereby, benefit yourself.

And you'll still be a *nice person*.

Mistake #3

NOT SAYING WHAT YOU WANT

> Friends want to treat you to your birthday dinner and an evening of entertainment. You'd love to go to your favorite restaurant and take in a first-run film you're dying to see, but you're afraid it's too costly or they may not like the movie. So you don't say anything and leave it up to them. And they surprise you. They take you to the local lanes for hamburgers and bowling. You are trying to become a vegetarian and you *hate* bowling. So you have an *un*happy birthday. And you end up steamed at both your friends and yourself.

As my father grew older, he typically began to repeat jokes and favorite stories from the past. Many times I heard the one about Mr. Greene who owned the local candy store where kids stopped on their way home from school. One day, the word got around that "ole man Greenie" was giving away free sour balls. That sounded good to two third-grade pals, who decided to check out the rumor. The proprietor nodded a greeting as they entered the store, but when they stood for some time before the big, round fishbowl filled with the colorful hard candies, he said nothing. Finally, one of the boys worked up the courage to ask if he could have one of the free balls. "No," Mr. Greene said sternly, "I don't give them to those who ask." The boys stood there stunned for a few moments, then finally the other kid piped up, "I didn't ask, Mr. Greene." The man looked down at him and said, "No, that's because you didn't want any."

Whether he knew it or not, my father's story identified one of the predicaments we nice people face when we want something from others. We're afraid that if we ask, they'll think we're pushy and won't give it to us; and if we don't ask, they'll assume we don't want it. Either way we won't get what we want.

Every day we have normal, appropriate needs and wants that other people are suited to meet. But in the moment when our desires are the strongest and the opportunity is the greatest, we simply don't express them. I'm talking about when we know what we want, when our desires are legitimate, and when we have immediate access to those who are able to fulfill them. Even if we're normally articulate, and we intuitively know we'll miss out on something important if we don't speak up, in certain social contexts our ability to express ourselves consistently stalls and shuts down. Unfortunately, we're usually not aware at the moment that something is blocking us, and that by our silence we are not functioning effectively. But even when we are, we usually don't realize what has gone wrong until the moment has passed.

TYPES OF TRANSACTIONS

Five types of social transactions give rise to this silence. Some are personal in nature, others are commercial. Some are pedestrian and seem to be of minor importance, while others we recognize as critical for our personal well-being. All of them are under the control of forces that frighten and diminish us.

THE TRANSACTION THAT WILL COST OTHERS SOMETHING

You don't ask a friend to pay for an expensive dinner for you on your birthday. Or say you know that your friendly neighbor works downtown near the bakery where you ordered a cake. He could easily pick it up and bring it home for you. You'd love to have him do that, but you don't want to impose. So you don't ask, and you take the ninety-minute round-trip drive on top of your busy schedule and pick it up yourself.

THE TRANSACTION WHERE WE'RE AFRAID THAT WHAT WE WANT WILL CAUSE CONFLICT

The thought of making people angry at us, of being thought rude, or of being turned down and embarrassed scares us. For example, you're a guest in someone's house and he's smoking. You have bronchial problems or simply hate the smell, but you're unwilling—or unable—to ask him not to smoke. Or you're at lunch in a restaurant where a child's misbehavior is upsetting you and everyone else. All of you would like the parents to do something (*anything, for crying out loud!*). But no one says a word.

The Transaction Where People Make a Mistake that Costs Us, or They Try to Take Advantage of Us

You treat a friend to dinner and the waitress brings a bill that looks several dollars too large. You become tense inside. You don't know whether she's padded the bill or made a mistake, but as a nice person you don't want to embarrass her or yourself, so you pay without asking for an explanation. Or a friend to whom you made a loan, repayment for which is now overdue, never mentions it, and you don't say anything either.

The Transaction Where an Insensitive Authority Figure or Bully Walks all over Us

Nasty people and strong authority figures intimidate us. We're convinced that confronting them won't do any good. You'd like the boss to stop shoving too much work on you, but you grind on under it in silence. Or your doctor hurriedly prescribes medicine that's never done you any good, and you don't say a thing.

The Transaction Where We Need or Want Something Intimate

Intimacy can be embarrassing, even excruciating. If we feel taken for granted by an indifferent spouse—particularly if it's gone on for years—we may find it too painful to mention. Or we may not be able to talk about our sexual desires with our mates. Your sex life may have become routine and you'd like to try something new, but when it comes time to make love you're unable to say so.

Because we don't feel we can ask for what we want, in any of these transactions we may unconsciously resort to tactics that are indirect. We may try to manipulate those who are involved, attempting to make them feel guilty, hoping to get what we want without having to ask directly for it. Or we may drop hints, expecting those close to us to read our minds and do what we want, even though we never tell them what it is. And if they don't figure it out on their own, we even may become angry at them. Whatever our ploy, we become indirect because we don't feel free to say directly what we want.

I had never been shy, but it was not until the midseventies that I saw the importance of telling people what I wanted from them. I had read about assertiveness, but I had never recognized the deficit in myself. Yet without being conscious of it, I was afraid of conflict, of appearing selfish, or of embarrassing myself or someone else, and these fears inevitably drove me either to keep quiet or be indirect in expressing my desires.

THE PROBLEM IN VARIOUS SOCIAL CIRCLES

In our urban world we experience at least five circles of relationships in which we don't ask for what we want, and where we pay a wide range of prices for our silence.

THE CIRCLE OF STRANGERS

These individuals mean little to us personally—the clerk in the big downtown store, our waitress while dining in a distant city, the person we pass on the street. As nice people, we treat them with civility and expect the same in return. That we don't tell them what we want is usually not a problem. If they attempt to take things that are ours, however, or if we need something from them and don't speak up, we lose things we deserve or to which we're entitled.

THE CIRCLE OF OCCASIONAL FUNCTIONARIES

We do business with these people now and then: the clerk at the cleaner's, our insurance agent, the teller at our bank, our auto mechanic or hairstylist. Our primary interest is not to know them better, but to have them serve us well. Yes, we're happy to be friendly with the clerk at the cleaner's, but we don't want to hear her life story or tell her ours; we want our jackets well cleaned and pressed. If we respectfully tell these people what we want, we usually get it.

THE CIRCLE OF IMPORTANT POWER PEOPLE

Here are our bosses, co-workers, clients, customers, and authority figures: physicians, attorneys, professors, pastors, etc. We may be on a first-name basis with them, but our relationships tend to be more official than personal. They are in position to exploit us on a regular basis, and if they abuse us we often must pay serious consequences. So we have a lot to gain by telling people with power exactly what we expect from them.

THE CIRCLE OF FRIENDS

This arena enfolds not only friends, but close neighbors, acquaintances, and fellow club or church members as well. They mean a good bit to us and are people we want to know better. When we don't tell them our desires, we experience them merely at the shallow level of exchanging pleasantries and courtesies. When we do tell them what we want, we inevitably feel closer to them.

THE CIRCLE OF INTIMATES

Our confidants include a spouse, sibling, favorite aunt, or a dear friend. Ideally, we let down our barriers before these people and relate with mutual honesty and trust. We tell them how much they mean to us, and from such exchanges we are deeply enriched. At one level, we want them to know everything about us. But the more intimate our desires, especially if they are unconventional, the more difficult it is to articulate them. And it's in this sphere that the consequences of our silence are most poignant and painful.

In our better moments, we know that we're entitled to certain things from the people in all of these circles—especially the last three—and that not to say what we want is a mistake. Yet, for several reasons, we continue not to speak up.

WHY DON'T WE SAY WHAT WE WANT?

WE BELIEVE IT IS SOCIALLY INAPPROPRIATE

Our parents taught us that nice people don't speak up for themselves, that we're supposed to look out for the interests of others, rather than our own. We learned that to ask for things we want is to be greedy or selfish. Of course, if what we wanted was socially acceptable or they had previously approved or promised it, we need only say *please*. But, indeed, they never taught us how to ask directly for something that wasn't a foregone conclusion.

WE DON'T WANT TO APPEAR WEAK

Nice parents often tell their children that real adults are strong and don't need help from others. So most of us nice people—particularly we men—tend to think that to need things from others is a sign of weakness. We have believed mistakenly that independence, rather than interdependence, is the adult psychology.

WE ARE UNEASY ABOUT THE LEGITIMACY OF OUR WANTS

As children we may have been scolded for desiring something and made ashamed of what we wanted. It was part of our treatment that generated our low sense of self-worth. So now as adults we often feel, rightly or wrongly, that our desires are excessive, wasteful, harmful, inappropriate, or simply things we have no right to expect from others.

WE'RE AFRAID OF REJECTION

Along with the first two mistakes—trying to be perfect and taking on too much—not saying what you want is a lifelong habit rooted in the fear of humiliation and abandonment. In childhood, our long-evolved, complex brain first alerted us to the social threat of possible rejection by people who are important to us. From our days as infants, this fear kept us from risking our security, our relationships, our inner core—what we prize the most. It helped us survive. Unfortunately, it also taught us to protect too much, to play it too safe, so our capacities for risk as adults are stunted and atrophied. Yes, when you learn you are accepted unconditionally at the center of life and accept your acceptance, you deal a blow to this fear and excessive self-protection. But even with this decision, the fear may not disappear altogether and may keep you from telling others what you want.

Has it come as a surprise that you regularly fail to express what you want from others and that such behavior is self-defeating? You probably recall when you didn't tell someone what you wanted, but it may never have dawned on you that you do it so consistently and that it's a serious mistake. Since you won't begin expressing your desires to others until you're convinced your silence is a mistake, look at several reasons why it is.

WHY OUR SILENCE IS A MISTAKE

IT RENDERS US UNKNOWN

When we don't express our desires we reveal to others only our personas, the images of ourselves we project to be socially acceptable. Thus we are only somewhat present to them and they only know us partially. An irony: We remain silent about what we want so as not to harm our relationships, and our silence makes them superficial.

WE DON'T KEEP FAITH WITH OUR OWN BEST INTERESTS

We have an essential human need to satisfy those desires that enable us to experience wholeness, that honor our worth as persons, and that help us as social beings to contribute appropriately to the common good. So to keep silent about our legitimate wants is to betray our integrity and our ability to live fully.

WE ASK FOR TREATMENT WE DON'T DESERVE

We allow others to assume we don't care about what is rightly ours. We invite them to take from us without giving back, to always leave the dirty work for us, to use us for their own ends. Our silence does not *cause* others to abuse us, but it becomes the occasion for it by providing them with the opportunity to get away with it.

WE WASTE ENERGY AND MAKE OURSELVES SICK

In order to keep quiet, we expend a great deal of emotional power we could be using to tell others what we need. We also burden ourselves with a lot of regret as we wonder, Why didn't I ask? In the end, we both resent those from whom we don't get what we want and are angry at ourselves for not speaking up. This anger, suppressed and turned inward, puts us in danger of depression and serious illness.

WE MISS OUT ON MUCH THAT WE DESERVE

In part, others don't respond to our wants simply because they're in the dark about them, or because they haven't been nudged into action by hearing us express them. Thus we go through life much poorer than is necessary. Indeed, our silence is self-defeating. The fact is, we can get much of what we deserve from others simply by letting them know what we want.

Here are specific steps that will help you begin to change your behavior.

INITIAL ACTIONS

1. Acknowledge that Not to Say What You Want Is a Self-Defeating Mistake

Accept the fact you have wronged yourself by your silence. Only when you see it as a mistake can you break the habit and begin to speak up.

2. Decide You're Not Going to Behave This Way Anymore

Say to yourself, From now on, I'm going to tell others what I want from them. Write it down, date it, and add it to the growing list of resolutions on your refrigerator.

3. Enlist the Support of Friends

Tell them you have a problem asserting yourself. (They probably already know it and have the same problem themselves.) Making yourself vulnerable in this way can elicit their willingness to be supportive. If your silence has harmed relationships with them in the past, you might cast your notice in apologetic terms. You might say, "I'm sorry, I've tended not to tell you what I want. Whether you know it or not, I've left you in the dark and undermined your ability to know me. I'm trying not to do that anymore."

These three actions do not insure that you'll automatically start speaking up. This habit dies hard. Central to the problem are three assumptions that spring from your training in niceness and have misled you all along. You need to replace them with alternative perspectives.

THREE IMPORTANT PERSPECTIVES

PERSPECTIVE ONE INSISTS ON A DIFFERENCE BETWEEN SELF-LOVE AND SELFISHNESS

Our parents taught us to be selfless and not to be selfish, to put others first all the time. So whenever we are about to do something for ourselves, even when we've been knocking ourselves out for others, we hear our inner voices tell us we're not being nice. We wrongly assumed that self-love and selfishness are one and the same. They're not. Look at what makes them different.

To be selfish is to be so preoccupied with ourselves that we are unable to consider the rights and needs of others. It is to so misunderstand our spiritual connection to others that we fail to see that the healthy relationships are based on giving as well as getting, including getting by *giving*.

We all know that children and adolescents in their insecurity have trouble moving beyond themselves to attain the equilibrium that healthy relationships require. They tend to be selfish. And until they attain maturity, which may not come until well into adult years—if ever—they pay the price for it. When they are preoccupied with themselves, paradoxically, they unconsciously endure their selfishness as a burden and cannot feel good about themselves. Selfishness is the style our parents wanted us to avoid, because it's neither nice nor smart.

In contrast, self-love is wise and a builder of self-worth. Self-love means that we neither insist on always taking care of ourselves first nor always defer to others. By definition, adults see themselves as social by nature and responsible to interdependence, the common good, and the law of love. Thus they love both themselves and others.

Self-love calls us to the delicate balance of loving others at the same time, in the same ways, and to the same extent that we love ourselves. This means that in any given moment, if we cannot serve both others and ourselves, we must choose whom to serve first. Sometimes it will be others because their needs outweigh ours, or because it's the right time, the right place, or their turn to have our attention. Sometimes our needs will be larger than theirs, or it will be our turn, so we'll put ourselves first and tell others what we want from them.

It's important to note that the self-interest inherent in self-love is natural and unavoidable. Whether we are selfish or achieve real depth and balance to our self-love, we cannot act contrary to what we think is in our interest—even when we're mistaken about what that is. And even when we sacrifice something for someone in an apparent transcendence of self-interest, it is not quite as grand as it appears. But it's also important to see that such self-interest is not selfish or unhealthy, but actually can contribute to our wholeness.

If you are willing to tell others what you want, you do not need to be selfish. You can pursue your own interests in ways that reflect a love of others and yourself. And isn't this exactly what you want from your relationships?

Perspective Two Says We Need to Be Fully Present to Those Who Are Important to Us

If you were raised to be nice, you probably were taught to put your best foot forward, to keep a stiff upper lip, never to let people see you sweat or cry. Thus you may have always believed it's too risky or impossible to be fully present to those you care about. Not so. And full presence is a major key to your personal wholeness. Look at what it means, why it's exactly what is needed in relationships, and how you can experience it.

We offer our full presence to those who matter to us when we're able to make ourselves vulnerable to them. Our vulnerability tells them we care about them, trust them, and value what they have to offer. Unfortunately, most of us, most of the time, do not let ourselves be vulnerable enough so that others can experience us completely. We carefully protect ourselves, stifling our emotions and holding back on telling them what we want. As a result we offer them only a part of who we are and render ourselves only partially present. So we usually do not feel close even to family and friends and often find ourselves and them emotionally absent. Thus we lose out on the richness others can add to our lives, and this loss contributes to our feeling of being incomplete.

At an immediate level, to be fully present is to reveal more to others than we communicate simply through appearances, facts and figures, and a socially adjusted, nice disposition. It means, among other things, that we let them know our ideas and feelings including our desires—

even those we're uneasy about. At a deeper level, it means being honest about our weaknesses and fears. Only when others know what we're afraid of and what we need can they know and relate to us as we really are.

In the late eighties, a man whose teenage son was using and selling drugs came to me. He was angry, but he also was in agony about what was happening to the boy and about the distance between them and their almost total lack of communication. He confessed he had always tried to maintain an image of being strong and perfect for his son. He also acknowledged that he was worried about his reputation in the business community and told me how hard it was to admit, even to himself, what his boy was doing. We talked about his fears and what was ultimately most precious to him. He finally was able to go to the son and say, "Because of you, I've been deathly afraid of being seen as a failure as a parent. My insecurities have gotten between us and I'm sick about it. But I love you and I'm afraid you'll ruin your life. I want you to get help immediately." For the first time in years he became present for his son. It led to a conversation that brought about their reconciliation and a slow but sure recovery for the boy.

I'm not suggesting that to be fully present to others you must tell them everything about yourself. At any time, they need to know those things that suit your relationship and pertain to the issue at hand, those things that will make you real to them at that moment. But even those closest to you do not need to know every lurid detail of your dark side, every grotesque fantasy you've ever had, everything you've ever done of which you were ashamed. Full presence requires **appropriate,** *but not inexhaustible,* **honesty.**

How we talk to others affects the degree to which we're present for them. If we say certain things in certain ways, our speech shields us from connecting with them deeply. If we use different terms, our words can render us open and known. It's important to know, however, that full presence is not first of all a strategy, a tactic, or a technique; it's a way of being in a relationship. In practical terms, it's the style of openness we create in all kinds of daily situations by being appropriately honest with others about how we feel and what we'd like from them. It's the trusting closeness we offer them on an ongoing basis through the genuineness of the most ordinary things we do. It's a different foundation for relationship than self-protection and is essential to our freedom to tell others what we want from them. And, of course, it's the state of being we are able to create most easily if we've accepted ourselves and have a realistic sense of our own worth. Once again we are reminded of the primary significance of receiving and giving unconditional acceptance.

There is more to full presence, some dimensions of which I'll address in the final chapter. At this point, however, it's enough to see that your personal fulfillment and the quality of your relationships depend on your commitment to it, and that such presence both requires you and frees you to tell others what you want from them.

PERSPECTIVE THREE IDENTIFIES AGGRESSION AND ASSERTIVENESS AS TWO DIFFERENT SOCIAL STYLES—ONE NEGATIVE, ONE POSITIVE

As nice people we have failed to distinguish between these styles and have viewed them both as negative.

Seeing the difference between them can help free us to tell others what we want. Look at how these two forms of expression differ:

> To be *aggressive* is to dominate people and take
> away their rightful power.
> To be *assertive* is to express your wants and
> leave their power intact.

> To be *aggressive* is to affirm only your own needs
> and worth.
> To be *assertive* is to affirm the worth of both
> others and yourself.

> To be *aggressive* is selfish.
> To be *assertive* expresses a healthy self-love.

We *assert* ourselves when we respectfully ask something of others that's appropriate. Rather than aggressively imposing our needs on them and turning them off, our assertiveness makes them feel needed and they find satisfaction in responding. Something beautiful can happen when we tell others what we want from them. In doing so, we actually honor them and deepen the bond between us. Simply seeing that assertiveness is a natural expression of self-love that enhances us and our relationships can help free us to tell others what we want.

To understand these three perspectives is important, but it is not enough. The freedom to express your desires to others will come only with your decision to live by them. Are you willing to love yourself? Be fully present to those you care about? Assert yourself in a respectful way?

If you answer yes to these questions, you're ready to begin developing an assertive behavioral style.

STEPS TOWARD AN ASSERTIVE STYLE

Family structures, social institutions, and governments exist to meet certain of your needs. And you, of course, must use them to support yourself. But to get all you deserve, you also must stand up to strangers, acquaintances, co-workers, authority figures, family members, and that person or two to whom you're the closest. Only then can you begin to fulfill your life.

Sometimes you'll want them to do something they haven't done before; sometimes you'll want them to stop doing something they have been doing. You cannot count on their insight and initiative to discern and meet your wishes. Instead, as a first step, you must consciously adopt and develop communication patterns that enable you to say clearly, directly, and compellingly what you want.

LEARN THE LANGUAGE OF HEALTHY ASSERTIVENESS

In asserting yourself, whether you want people to stop or start doing something, you need to be *positive, specific*, and *direct* rather than *negative, indirect, manipulative,* or *moralistic*.

Such compelling assertions, because they are clear, honest, and respectful, tend to make others want to give you what you desire and deserve. On the other hand, if you're negative, you create negative responses; if you're indirect, you burden others with explaining themselves; if you're manipulative, you make them resentful and resistant; if you're moralistic, you force them to act out of obligation and guilt. Here are examples of healthy assertiveness alongside of, and in contrast to, how unhealthy communications sound:

When You Want Children to Pick up Their Toys

I'd like you to pick up your toys. (Or, *Will you please pick up your toys?*)
 Not,
Don't leave your toys lying around. (Negative)
 Not,
Why don't you pick up your toys? (Negative and indirect)
 Not,
You shouldn't leave your toys lying around. (Negative and moralistic)
 Not,
Nice kids don't leave their toys lying around. (Negative, indirect, manipulative)

When You Want Your Loved One to Bring You Flowers

I'd like you to bring me flowers now and then. (Or, *Please bring me flowers once in a while.*)
 Not,
Don't forget to bring me flowers. (Negative)
 Not,
Why don't you bring me flowers anymore? (Negative and indirect)
 Not,
You ought to bring me flowers now and then. (Moralistic)

Not,
Nice spouses/lovers don't forget to bring their partners flowers. (Negative, indirect, manipulative)

When You Want Others to Take Care of Their Dishes

I'd like you to put your dishes in the dishwasher. (Or, *Will you please put your dishes in the machine?*)
Not,
Don't leave your dirty dishes in the sink.
(Negative)
Not,
Why don't you put your dishes in the dishwasher?
(Negative and indirect)
Not,
You should put your dishes in the dishwasher.
(Moralistic)
Not,
Considerate people don't leave their dirty dishes lying around. (Negative, indirect, manipulative)

When You Want to Be Held

I'd like you to hold me. (Or, *Will you please hold me for a moment?*)
Not,
I shouldn't have to tell you every time I want to be held. (Negative)
Not,
Why don't you hold me? (Negative and indirect)
Not,
You ought to hold me at a time like this.
(Moralistic)
Not,

Caring people hold those they love at times like these. (Indirect and manipulative)

If you are having trouble understanding the difference between healthy and unhealthy assertiveness, reverse the social transaction—imagine someone else telling you what they want in these different ways, and see what feelings it generates in you. Here are more illustrations of healthy assertiveness:

I'd like you to be positive, specific, and direct
　　with me.
I want you to talk respectfully to me.
I love you and I want you to come home.
I want you to start spending only the money you
　　have.
I'd like you to be in on the decision about the
　　car.
Will you please take the cleaning with you when
　　you leave?
I'd like you to chair the committee.
I'd like you to touch me like this, right here,
　　right now.

When alone, you can practice asserting yourself. Start with little wants. Put yourself mentally in the kinds of transactions we've been talking about and tell imaginary people what you'd like from them. Talk to yourself, repeating lines like those above until they begin to feel natural and spontaneous. You'll soon be expressing your wants with confidence and ease and be able to move to the larger, more intimidating matters. And as a result, you'll not only get what you want more often, but you'll also enrich your relationships.

TRACK DOWN THE FEAR THAT'S BLOCKING YOU, AND NAME IT

It's fear that dictates your silence. Stay with the moment and concentrate on feeling your fear. Ask yourself, What am I afraid of? What's scaring me half to death? Listen to your inner voices until they tell you. Because you don't like to feel afraid, you may not be able to hear them right away.

A woman sat down with me one day to talk about a co-worker. She respected this person and knew he thought highly of her. But he wasn't doing his part on the important project she was in charge of, and she didn't know how to approach him. I asked her what she was afraid of, and after a minute she said, "I'm afraid he'll think I'm a slave driver and won't like me." I asked, "What else?" "Well," she said, "of course I'm afraid that if he doesn't do his part, the thing will flop and it will ruin my reputation." I asked her if she thought she could say to him, "I'm afraid you'll think I'm a slave driver and won't like me, but I'm also afraid that if you don't do your part, this thing will flop and I'm going to get all the blame. I want you to hold up your end of the bargain on our project." She decided she could, that's what she did, he apologized, they both felt better about working together, and they not only did a terrific, satisfying job, but they also both received a great deal of recognition for it.

Whenever you become aware of not speaking up, it may help to make a list of your possible fears until you isolate the one that is stopping you. First, admit it to yourself, and then express it to the one from whom you want something. If you find you're afraid of:

- **Embarrassing yourself:** "I'm embarrassed to ask this, but I would like you to do such-and-such for me."
- **Disapproval:** "I'm afraid that were I to tell you what I want, you may not like me anymore."
- **Being seen as pushy:** "I'd like you to do something for me, but I'm afraid you'll think I'm pushy."

WHEN YOU'RE AFRAID YOU'LL BE SEEN AS PUSHY, ASK FOR INFORMATION

Encounters that render you silent occur in unpredictable situations where facts often are new, unclear, or change quickly. So you'll often be uncertain about the realities that are shaping the situation and about your rights. To assert yourself effectively is not to blurt out immediately what you want, but to clarify what is happening, what is available to you, and what your rights are. So your first task may be to become informed by asking questions. And the very asking may get you what you deserve.

I took my car in for some engine work and brake shoes. I forgot the discount coupons they sent me in the mail. When I told my mechanic, he said he would have them knock $40 off my bill anyway. (He knows me as a good customer.) Later, when I went to pay the cashier, no discount had been taken. I couldn't insist they give it to me—I forgot my coupons—but I had been counting on the mechanic's word and forty bucks is forty bucks. Rather than make a fuss or remain silent and walk away frustrated and angry, I went back to the mechanic and politely asked if I was confused about the discount. He might have said yes, or that he had misinformed me and was sorry. If he had, there was little I could have done. But he didn't. He apologized for not telling the cashier and then saw to it that $40 was cut from my bill. I got what I wanted without being pushy. It doesn't hurt to ask for information.

PRACTICE PERSISTENCE

In certain transactions you may face resistance. Even when you're thoughtful, positive, and direct about what you want, some people will be unwilling—at least at first—to give it to you, and you'll need to stand your ground. Children, for instance, can be very resistant.

YOU: Please pick up your toys now, before dinner; you'll be too tired to do it later.

CHILD: I'll do it after dinner. I want to play a little longer.

YOU: I know you want to play. I want you to pick up before dinner.

CHILD (*pouting*): I don't want to do it now. I'll do it after dinner.

YOU: I know you don't want to do it now, but I want you to.

CHILD (*making a face, stomping a foot*): No. I want to play until dinner.

YOU: You'll be too tired to put them away after dinner, I want you to do it now.

CHILD: Oh, all right.

You also may have to be persistent when strong adults, particularly authority figures, resist the idea of giving you what you deserve. When Barbara and I were first married, I was in school and she worked as a nurse for a prominent doctor who paid his professional staff poorly. We were intimidated by him, so we never expressed our important feelings or told him what we wanted. And over the two years she worked for him, she never received a cent for overtime.

Years ago, the physicians' mystique vanished for me. I started to see doctors as human beings, and while I continue to respect those who do good work and care about their patients, I no longer deify them. And I'm now quite persistent with them about receiving information and treatment that are rightly mine.

In July of '93, the results of my Prostate Specific Antigen (PSA) blood test suggested, among other things, the possible presence of prostate cancer. My primary care physician referred me to a urologist, who had me take an ultrasound test. While I was on the table, the picture on the screen showed a hard, cashew-shaped something or other right in the middle of my prostate. He told me it was a tumor. He then said he wanted to biopsy it and do ten other needle probes to check the entire prostate, and, "Since we're already in there, we might as well do it now." I agreed.

When we finished, he told me to make another appointment for the next Tuesday, and he'd have the lab results on the biopsies. It was Friday morning, and Barbara and I, with our four children and their families, were on our way to two weeks' vacation, five hours away. I told him this and asked him to phone me there on Tuesday. He didn't want to do that.

DOCTOR: I don't usually give test results on the phone.

I:	It may not be normal practice, but I want you to make an exception. I don't want to spend a day of my vacation running back and forth.
DOCTOR:	I don't like to give results on the phone, especially when the news might be bad.
I:	I understand your reluctance, but whether the news is good or bad, I'd like you to call me on Tuesday.
DOCTOR:	Why don't you plan to see me as soon as you get back?
I:	No, I don't want to fret about this for two weeks. I'd like you to call me.
DOCTOR:	The results may not be in until Wednesday, when I'll be in surgery.
I:	Then I'd like you to call me when you've finished surgery.
DOCTOR:	I suppose I could do it then.
I:	Thank you. Let me give you the number where I'll be.

He called early in the afternoon the next Thursday. He said, "I'm sorry to tell you that the news is not as good as I had hoped for." I felt a stab in my stomach. He asked, "Do you remember the tumor we saw on the ultrasound screen?" "Yes," I said. He went on: "No problem. It's a benign, fibrous cyst." My stomach relaxed for a moment. "But," he continued, "two of the needle probes picked up cancer down low on the backside of your prostate." Tight stomach again. I told him, "That isn't the news I wanted to hear," and he said, "I understand." We agreed that I'd come and see him when I got home so we could talk about my options, and I thanked him for calling. After I put down the phone, Barbara and I stood for some time holding one another, trembling a bit, unable to say much, our eyes moist. And then we had a week to be alone with one another and our children and to process something of what this would mean—an experience we would have missed if I had not been persistent with the urologist. Two months later, he removed the prostate, and tests so far show that the surgery apparently did the trick.

When I talk about persisting on behalf of what you want, I'm not suggesting you browbeat those who are unresponsive to your requests. I'm saying that when you ask for something reasonable, you owe it to yourself not to take no for an answer the first time around. This will require you to stay focused on what you want, to reflect back what you think they're saying (and feeling), and repeat your interest as often as needed.

Of course, even when you tell others repeatedly what you want from them, it doesn't mean they'll give it to you. But at least they'll know who you are. You also won't have to forever wonder whether you would have gotten it if you had asked. In addition, you can use the rejection as a point of growth. Trying to take care of your own legitimate interests is a mark of maturity. But so is learning to deal creatively with disappointment. Both are stepping-stones on the journey toward maturity, as well as signs that, in some measure, you have arrived.

It must also be said that a healthy, persistent assertiveness may come back to bite you. In the mid-eighties, our daughter, going through a divorce, came with her darling little girl to live at our house while she herself finished college. Cast in the role of surrogate father to our granddaughter, I decided it was important to model assertive behavior (I wasn't good at it when her mother was a child but I had worked on my skills). As soon as she could understand, I would say things like, "It's time for dinner, I would like you to pick up your toys," or "I want you to listen to your mother." She responded beautifully. Very seldom did I have to repeat myself. I always referred to her in public as the "Most Wonderful Little Girl in All the World" (grandparents will relate to this).

When she was five, early on Easter Sunday—a busy and stressful time for me—she opened the door of my study and said, "Beebop [her affectionate name for Grandpa], I want you to come see my beautiful new dress." I said, "I'd love to, sweetface, but I'm very busy. I'll see it in a little while." She turned and left. Soon she was back, tugging on my sleeve: "Beebop, I want you to come *now* and see my beautiful dress." I said, "As soon as I can, honey. I have to finish what I'm doing." Again, she left abruptly. And again in a few minutes, she was back and, this time, seeing I was still engrossed in my work, she pushed her way onto my lap and into my face, cupping my chin in her hands so I had to look her straight in the eyes, and said loudly, **"Beebop, I know you're busy, but I want you to see my beautiful new dress *right now!*"**

I had taught her well. I got a dose of my own persistence medicine. I went immediately to see her dress.

INVITE OTHERS TO SAY WHAT THEY WANT FROM YOU

Almost all nice people have difficulty expressing their desires. Whenever you see that others are intimidated by you, you can encourage them to speak up. You can say, "Your feelings are important to me." Assure them you'll consider their requests. Then listen.

Yes, they may ask for things you don't want to give them or they have no right to expect. But if you deem their wants unhealthy or illegitimate, or you think they're being unfair or excessive, you can tell them: "I'm sorry, you're asking too much of me and I'm not going to do it." Even while turning them down, you can express your appreciation for their candor in telling you what they want. And, at any time, if you sense it is hard for them to express their interests, you can say: "I know it's not easy for you to ask."

Inviting those close to you to be assertive has several pluses. For one, it encourages them to integrate their words with their true desires, enabling them to be more integrated and liberated and more interesting company. It also can create a climate of respect and trust between you and them that makes for relationships that are more enriching. Then, too, it can remind you of your own continuing need to assert yourself and, if it liberates them to be assertive, their behavior can provide you with a model for your own. In other words, your consideration of their need to say what they want, paradoxically, can benefit you.

YOU NOW HAVE WAYS TO SAY WHAT YOU WANT

You may be saying to yourself, I don't want to stifle my basic needs and legitimate desires anymore—I want to begin to say what I want. You still, of course, will face social situations that have made you tongue-tied in the past, and to master assertiveness skills may take some time. But deliberate practice will pay off. And you at least can get started:

- When you want something from people, you can tell them directly in positive, nonmoralistic terms, "I would like you to . . ."
- When you find you're afraid to be assertive, you can identify your fear for those involved: "I'm afraid you'll think I'm pushy, but will you . . ."
- When you're uncertain about what you have a right to expect from others, you can ask for information: "Pardon me, but can you tell me if you offer . . ."
- When someone resists giving you what you want and deserve, you can dig in and press for it: "I know you are resisting me, but I want you to . . ."
- When people are intimidated by you, you can encourage them to tell you directly what they want: "I want you to tell me what you want from me; I don't want you to be afraid."

Practicing these steps will not only make you more aware of when you're not saying what you want, but it also will help you develop your own assertive style. In certain situations you still may find yourself afraid to express your desires. But with practice this will happen less and less as the days go by. Moreover, to assert yourself appropriately will become increasingly easier over time, and your relationships will be ever more satisfying.

And you'll still be a *nice person*.

Mistake #4
SUPPRESSING ANGER

Your boss skirts company policy in such a way that he robs you of a large commission you were counting on. You are livid, but you say nothing. You take your anger home from the office and spew it all over your spouse and the dining room table. During dessert, while you are still fuming, the boss calls on a minor matter of unrelated business. And you immediately sound as sweet as Mr. Rogers.

Many years ago, long before I stopped thinking of doctors as gods, I hurried to my internist's office for a routine physical checkup. I was scheduled for two in the afternoon and arrived right on time. When twenty minutes passed and I was still reading old magazines, I tapped on the receptionist's window and politely asked her how long she thought it would be. She said, "Not long," and I took her words at face value. Fifteen minutes later I asked her if she knew what the delay was. "The doctor hasn't gotten back from lunch but should be along shortly." I was irked, but waited for a half hour more before she took me to one of those sterile little procedure rooms. I sat in my shorts for another fifteen minutes and could feel my stomach continue to tighten, but I kept my cool. When the doctor finally entered—at almost three-thirty—he mumbled something about being sorry for the delay. And I said, "That's okay."

When I talk about anger, I'm referring to the inner displeasure we all experience when we think others have threatened, exploited, or in some way abused us, plus our urge to retaliate. It's the emotion that prepares us to strike back whenever we're offended. In one sense, to live is to be angry, for from the moment we're born, everyone else impinges on our interests. Since life at its most primitive and intimate levels is a competitive struggle for territory and survival, we constantly feel like we're being invaded or violated.

Anyone can make us angry. Some of us are still resentful about things our parents did to us when we were children. We become irritated when people press us to do things we don't want to do or don't give us what we want. Even when we fall head over heels in love and are blinded by bliss, the object of our affection sooner or later does something to infuriate us. And, of course, we often harbor anger at ourselves.

We're also angered by impersonal matters over which we have little control, such as the weather and the world at large. We get rankled by people and institutions that treat others unjustly or rape the environment, whether they do it intentionally or not. The opposite sex may make us angry. And deep down, the awareness that the eventual cost of life is death makes us resentful. The fact is, we're angry a lot of the time, about a lot of things, and with a lot of people, including those we love the most.

Some of us, of course, are angrier than others. And the displeasures all of us feel at given times vary dramatically in intensity. We call the mild forms annoyance, irritation, and irk. The stronger ones we give names like indignation, resentment, wrath, fury, and rage. At the risk of oversimplifying a complex emotion about which we still know too little, I'm narrowing my focus to anger that is neither chronic nor necessarily excessive in passion, but that is regularly triggered when people step on us in some way—everyday anger that threatens us and the relationships we care so much about.

If you're a thoughtful and typically sensitive nice person, of course, you don't like to be angry, especially with someone who is important to you. You look on it as immature or wrong and think you ought to be above it all. Thus you may get angry with yourself for getting angry, and feel like less of a person for it. You even may apologize for getting angry. Yet all the while, as you well know, your niceness does not make you immune to anger. And every day, people in your life do things that tick you off:

- Your boss takes a commission you earned.
- A roommate leaves her dirty dishes for you to wash.
- Your brother speeds recklessly with you in his car.
- A friend puts you down repeatedly in front of your other friends.
- A neighbor cares for your place while you're away and doesn't feed the cat.

- Your spouse pays too much attention to someone else at a party.
- Someone accuses you of denying you're angry.

And whenever you become angry at people who are important to you, you menace your well-being as a social creature. If your anger gets out of control, or you deliberately unload it, you can ruin those relationships, your security on the job, and perhaps even your very life. So that doesn't happen to you, this chapter will help you find constructive ways to respond to people who are important to your life and who make you angry. First, though, it's important to understand that merely becoming angry is not in itself a mistake.

WHY GETTING ANGRY IS NOT
A MISTAKE

Anger is not a mistake. A mistake is a bad choice and we do not usually choose to get angry. No one had to teach us how. Anger goes off inside us automatically, without our permission. Whenever someone steps on us, our feelings and chemistry instantly do battle with our brains and prepare us to retaliate. Adrenaline immediately releases into the bloodstream and our blood-sugar concentration rises, electrically charging both us and the atmosphere around us. Unfortunately, there's much we don't understand about anger, and both scientific findings as well as our firsthand conclusions about it are often confusing and controversial. But everyone knows what it is to have this emotional response system flash and roar into action.

Mistake #4: Suppressing Anger

Second, the interpersonal anger we're concerned with is not a mistake because it springs essentially from our innate sense of what is right. Those who violate us arouse what some call our *judicial sentiment*. This emotional response, while refined and directed by our societies in line with their self-protective norms, comes built in, imbedded in our genes right along with our sex, our size, and the color of our eyes. It makes us shout, "That's wrong!" or "Not fair!" It knows—and tells us—that persons and institutions are responsible for their actions and ought not to abuse us. The displeasure we experience as a result of their violations is natural and normal—and may be justified—and cannot, therefore, in and of itself be seen as a mistake. (We'll deal with unjustified anger later.) Consider a basic example:

> A four-year-old's older sister swipes his favorite toy and his internal alarm goes off. He screams and stomps his feet and may even bite her. He's angry, not because he's selfish or simply wants to enjoy his own toy at the moment, although both may be true, but because what she did is unfair and she ought not to get away with it. His sense of justice has been offended and has registered a guilty verdict, and even though he's only four, when his parents fail to punish his sister and make her return his toy, without hesitation, he judges them guilty as well.

No one had to tell this kid he's worthy of respect and ought not to be walked on. No one taught him that his parents shouldn't let his big sister take advantage of him. Both his hair-trigger anger impulse alarm and his judicial sentiment created an appropriate indignation. We may see any biting he does as unsuitable and ultimately self-destructive, but since his anger arises from having his rights, his sense of fair play, his property, and his very person violated, we cannot label it a mistake.

Third, anger can't be a mistake because it helps us reach legitimate, worthwhile goals. It drives us to keep going when we're discouraged. It can assist us in changing the way others treat us, resonating with their built-in sense of fairness, compelling them to apologize and stop their abusive behavior. And this, of course, is what we deserve and want. And it follows that if we don't express our anger, we nice people encourage others to continue violating us.

Finally, we cannot call anger a mistake because, by its hopeful vision of justice, it has given birth to some of the world's greatest literature and art, creating beauty and meaning and hope in the midst of human melancholy and misery. It also helps transform the political realm by empowering people to protest unjust powers. The fact is, much of the positive social change in this world is accomplished by people who are angry because they have recognized injustice or actually felt the pain of those who have been wronged. And comparable to what happens at the one-to-one level, when we fail to demonstrate our outrage at social indifference and injustice, we exert no restraining influence on society's tendencies toward tyranny, corruption, and brutality.

While the intensity and immediacy of our anger generally scare us, it is important to see that being angry is not only normal and universal, it is also often beneficial. All of us can see that anger creates beauty and social good, including the repair and redesign of our relationships. Those of us acquainted with the history of religions know that the gods who have any character at all get angry when they hear about injustice, exploitation, and the various forms of personal abuse. The argument here is contrary to what we learned as children: **It's not a mistake to get angry; it's a mistake to think that anger is a mistake.** And as long as we view our anger through the eyes of our learned niceness, we will fail to recognize—and inevitably set ourselves up to make—the mistake all nice people make with their anger.

OUR MISTAKE WITH ANGER

While anger by definition is an emotional experience, not an activity, the mistake niceness dictates regarding our anger has to do with how we process it.

First, look briefly at how not-so-nice people tend to express their anger:

- *You dummy, get the hell out of my seat!*
- *I resent your saying that, you stupid moron!*
- *Stop cheating, you jerk! Get to the back of the line!*
- *I deserved that commission, you SOB. I'm outta here!*

As nice persons we may feel like letting off steam like this on occasion, but we don't—if we can help it—for several reasons. There may be heinous crimes that call for blatant bursts of outrage, but in the normal course of daily encounters we believe we cannot insult people and maintain either our dignity or satisfying relationships with them. We see such venting as self-serving and damaging to both individuals and a healthy social climate. We are aware, too, that it aggravates tense situations and may trigger violent reactions that could have devastating consequences. We also know that anger on any given occasion may be unjustified and that if we express it spontaneously we may embarrass ourselves.

Further, we realize that to react explosively is premature. Anger does not usually stay hot very long, but it cools quickly. Who hasn't been grateful on occasion when overpowered by a rush of rage, that a higher center in our brain shuts down the anger mode and kicks us into a mellower one? We may have felt at first like acting violently—"I could have killed him!"—which would have been disastrous, but somehow, fortunately, something in us, something of our better selves, took over and we calmed ourselves down.

So we do everything we can to avoid engaging in the tirades of not-so-nice people, for a number of reasons:

- We were taught by our parents that tantrums are childish and unacceptable.
- We associate such behavior with meanness.
- We don't want to model such behavior for the children we care about.
- We may have scruples about the harm disrespectful anger causes.
- We're terrified of what others might do if we act in such a manner.

Indeed, as nice people we don't willingly unleash our anger in nasty ways. We make the opposite mistake: **We do everything we can to suppress it.**

WHY SUPPRESSING ANGER IS A MISTAKE

IT MAKES US FALSE PEOPLE

We're hot as blazes and we try to look cool. We deny our feelings and pretend they aren't there. We do this even though we know that personal integrity and authentic relationships require that what we feel inside and what we communicate to others be one and the same. So our suppressed anger makes us feel untrue to ourselves as well as others, unworthy of our humanity, and, ironically, more angry.

IT SMOLDERS INTO A SELF-DEFEATING HATE

When a friend makes us angry and we don't express it, it kills the friendship. If the boss promotes others because they're younger and better looking, and we try to bury our anger, it festers to the point where we begin to hate both our boss and the work we've always enjoyed.

IT DOESN'T TRANSFORM OR FREE US FROM OUR DESTRUCTIVE URGE TO RETALIATE

Revenge, no matter how far down we push it, does not stay buried, let alone die. While buried, it saps our mental energy, poisons our well-being, and distracts us from moving on with our lives. And then, sooner or later, with all the power we felt when it first arose, it works its way out in any of four destructive ways:

1. Overkill

A friend snubs us and we explode out of proportion to what he did. We've been seething about a number of things, some of which are unrelated to him. But when he ticks us off, Boom! He doesn't deserve all that steam, but he gets the entire blast.

2. Indirection

A co-worker outperforms us and makes sure everyone knows it. We're embarrassed and fuming, but we say nothing. Without realizing it, we begin to make snide, sarcastic digs at her, we stall responses to her requests, and, in spite of our niceness, we may even stoop to backstabbing.

3. Misdirection

Our boss falsely accuses us of laziness. We want to strike at him, but we value our jobs and want everyone at work to think we're nice. So we vent our anger at home. We even run the danger of letting it escalate into violence against those we love.

4. Physical Illness

The medical community tells us that when we're chronically angry or don't express our negative emotions over time, we run the danger of creating serious health problems for ourselves: repeated headaches, heart disease, ulcers, depression, and other illnesses. In the long run, when we suppress our anger, it can kill more than our relationships; it can kill us.

Sadly, the most poignant toll taken by unspent anger occurs between nice people who care deeply about each other. For instance, spouses work hard at their jobs or become preoccupied with their children or the community and ignore their mates, taking their love for granted. These mates, then, even when they may understand the pressures and conflicting loyalties their spouses face, become angry about the indifference and loneliness they suffer. Believing their anger is unacceptable, however, they suppress it. They don't dare think about their hurt and resentment, let alone mention it to their spouses. It then manifests itself in one of the four destructive ways mentioned above or becomes an ongoing, low-grade hostility that dampens their affection, ruins their sex life, and drives a wedge between them and their spouses. If this happens, sooner or later they lose all of the emotional closeness, all of the intimacy in making love, all of the shared pleasures they once knew and that marriage is supposed to offer.

Think of it this way: No matter how good your intentions are, you don't forever control or destroy your anger by suppressing it—it controls and destroys you. And, whether you're attentive or not, the day inevitably comes when you learn, in one way or another, that you've made a serious mistake.

As a nice person, you need a new way to process your anger.

A CONSTRUCTIVE WAY TO PROCESS ANGER

When people anger you in normal, day-to-day social transactions, they need to know it. Face-to-face interchange with them about it will not only free you from emotional suffocation and allow you to be real; it will make authentic relationship with them possible. But there are four things to do before you bring your anger to their attention. If you make these moves, they will help you to be true to your feelings, to avoid being mean, and to keep your important relationships intact.

A. ACKNOWLEDGE AND ACCEPT YOUR ANGER WHEN IT ARISES

When your alarm goes off, whether a mild ring of irritation or a loud blast of rage, it's telling you you're angry. Listen to it. Hear the noise it makes inside you. Feel the heat it generates. Then stand back as if to see yourself in a mirror and say something like this to yourself: Hey! I'm *hot* about this. Like it or not, I feel *really angry!* Whoa, this *does tick me off!*

To acknowledge your anger right away allows you to experience and own it, which is critical for working it through and rising above it. Doing this may be difficult at first, because rather than embracing your anger as a gift of power, you've always suppressed it for fear of the consequences, especially of rejection. Yes, if you've accepted yourself by accepting your acceptance, you've reduced and perhaps largely eliminated this fear. But when your alarm sounds, you still may suppress both your anger and your fear out of habit. Your task now, instead, is immediately to admit and accept your anger—both your displeasure and your desire for retaliation. *A is for acceptance.*

B. BORROW TIME TO GATHER YOUR COMPOSURE

Sudden anger interferes with the brain's ability to make sense of things and *act smart*. If your head is in a spin and your insides in turmoil, do the old counting exercise. Relax for a moment. Take a long, deep breath. As you exhale, count slowly to yourself—*One-two-three-four*—until you can feel yourself settle down. If you find that you're in danger of being controlled by thoughts of striking back, tell yourself, *Stop!* Cut these thoughts off before they get a hold on you, by immediately rejecting them. You'll be surprised not only at how much easier you handle any temper you have, but also at how well it clears the way to express your anger constructively.

As you get used to composing yourself this way, you'll cut down on how high you need to count and on the time it takes you to express your anger. But here's the point: There's no need to be in a big hurry. Your basic purpose is to understand and control your feelings of vengeance rather than let them control you. And calming yourself for a few moments to let the intense heat dissipate is not the same as storing your anger. You simply control it temporarily to avoid a hasty, overblown, spontaneous response that could deal a fatal blow to a valued friendship or working relationship.

While counting, think of yourself as an observer and ask yourself these kinds of questions:

What's going on here? Why am I angry? How intense is my anger?

Is what I'm feeling based mostly on my sense of
what's right, or on lesser concerns?
What do I want to do with this anger? Is this the
right time and place to express it? How am I
going to talk about it?

The very act of pondering these questions can help
you get beyond the emotionally charged present to the
moment when you can talk calmly and directly about
your anger with the one who offended you.

Focusing yourself with these questions also gives
you a chance to discern whether your anger is justified.
If in these first few moments of reflection you pinpoint
where your anger comes from and see it isn't valid, you
can give it up and save yourself embarrassment, regret,
and possibly a friendship or a job, just because you
haven't lost your temper.

Again, to pause to get your bearings is not to cover
your anger forever. You *will* express it, but first you'll
determine how to edit potentially destructive remarks
and communicate your anger in a healing way.
Borrowing time allows you to think about it before you
express it, in contrast to the popular acting out, where
you act first and think about it later.

You will be careful with your anger because, while
you do not see yourself as responsible *for* others, you
sense a responsibility *to* them. You realize that they live
in you and you live in them, they are worth a great
deal to you, imperfect as they are—just like you—and
it's up to you as well as them to make the worlds you
live in as respectful and safe for one another as possible. *B is for borrowing time.*

C. CREATE MORE DISTANCE, IF NECESSARY

You may need more distance if the time and place aren't conducive to talking, if your anger alarm throws you out of control and you can't gain your composure, or if you're simply afraid you won't handle your anger well. You can say

> What you did upset me. I don't want to lose control, so let me get back to you. I want us to settle this amicably.
>
> I'm not sure what's going on, but I feel hurt and angry and I need time to calm down. I'd like to talk about this later.

To say "I *feel* hurt and angry," is direct but a bit softer than "I *am* hurt and angry." It will tend to provoke a smaller reaction. Keep in mind that anger is upsetting to just about everyone. Our four-year-old cannot borrow time, collect his composure, create distance, or reflect and communicate in this more sensitive and mature manner. But you can learn to do it. And each time you manage it, the more quickly you'll muster your courage and be confident the next time and the more you'll see yourself making progress. And the more progress you see you're making, the better you'll feel about yourself. *C is for creating the necessary distance.*

D. DECIDE WHAT TO SAY AND WRITE IT DOWN

Once you've gotten your bearings, identify what you do and *do not* want to say. You also may want to anticipate what you'll say if the person's reactions surprise and upset you further. Then jot down your responses and rehearse them. This will give you the best chance to say what you want to say and elicit constructive responses.

It also helps to decide when and where you will approach the person and what the inflection and tone in your voice will suggest. Whether you talk face-to-face—which is best but not always possible—or on the phone, you can keep your notes in front of you. Either way, you might plan to begin by saying, "Our relationship is important to me. I have done some thinking about what happened and about my reaction, and I want our conversation to be profitable, so I've made some notes."

When you write things down, the act itself helps clarify what you want to accomplish and how precisely to respond. It also helps your chances of defusing some of the distracting, excess heat that anger usually generates. *D is for deciding what you'll say.*

So from now on, when someone who is important to you makes you angry, rather than putting a permanent lid on your anger, you will:

Accept the fact that you are angry.
Borrow time to gather your composure.
Create the necessary distance.
Decide what you'll say and write it down.

EXPRESSING YOUR ANGER

Having come to terms with the fact that you're angry and gotten control of your anger, you're now ready to process it effectively.

STEP 1: EXPRESS IT DIRECTLY TO THOSE WHO VIOLATE YOU

To avoid the discomfort of conflict and possible retaliation, nice people often tell others about the violation, rather than the one who did it:

> I'm telling you, she's lied to me again and I'm steamed!
>
> It just kills me when he treats my sister that way!
>
> I can't believe how she talked about me in the office!

When people violate you, blowing your stack to others deprives the offenders of the opportunity to reply to your anger. It also does nothing to resolve your vengeful feelings or repair your relationships. In contrast, if you process your anger directly to those who offend you in the ways we'll come to shortly, you accomplish several things: You harmonize your actions with your feelings; you lessen your destructive desire for revenge; you increase your chances of getting them to stop abusing you; and you feel better about yourself.

In expressing your anger to those who violate you, it's appropriate to find the right moment and place to be alone with them. Only in the rarest of situations is it fitting or helpful to voice your anger at someone in front of others. And it normally serves both parties to negotiate a mutually acceptable time and neutral ground, if possible, so neither of you has an unfair advantage.

Of course, it's possible that talking face-to-face may

not be feasible due to geographical distance, conflicting schedules, or for other reasons. A letter may have to do, which is not all bad. Writing has the advantage of letting you reflect, edit, and rewrite until you get it right. A hard copy also can come in handy if you're misunderstood or later misquoted. Another idea: If a trusted friend has communication skills—and you won't be violating a confidence by talking about what happened—you might ask for feedback on the letter before you send it.

STEP 2: TALK FIRST ABOUT YOUR FEAR

When people make you angry you may experience disappointment, hurt, frustration, or some other negative emotion, but you always can count on fear being present. More than likely, you push this fear down inside, as well as your anger. Your task—just as when fear stops you from saying what you want—is to raise it to awareness and pinpoint its cause. Reflect on it. Perhaps you're afraid people might hurt you if they know you're angry with them. Maybe they'll tell your friends you're a bad person. They might block a promotion or a raise, or get you fired. And, even if you're close to them, they might become abusive or go so far as to sever their relationship with you. All of these possibilities are scary.

Deep down you know that those who truly care for you won't withdraw their love if you express anger. Yet even with them you may be afraid of the reaction it could create. Moreover, you may be afraid of the fear itself—afraid to feel it, afraid to express it, afraid even to acknowledge it. The idea here is to identify the cause of your fear and then **talk about it** *before* **you get to the anger.** If you can find the courage to do this, it will benefit you in several ways:

It Will Build Confidence and Character in You

When you suppress your anger and fear, or you simply tell others you're angry when you're also afraid, you are untrue to yourself and them. On the other hand, if you acknowledge both your fear and your anger, you are *fully honest, fully present, fully yourself,* and you develop character, that is, the moral, ethical, and spiritual quality that enables you to feel and act like yourself.

It Will Let You Feel Good about Yourself and What You've Done

When you realize you're dishonestly hiding your fear and anger, you feel guilty about it because you want to be a nice person. Your guilt in turn makes you angry at yourself, and self-anger leads to embarrassment and perhaps depression. But when you express both your fear and anger, you feel energized by your own honesty and enriched by growth in character.

It Will Make It Easier to Express Your Anger

To mention your fear first is to make yourself vulnerable, the opposite of coming on like a judge from a superior position. Humility and candor tend to elicit a sympathetic response, in contrast to the defensive retaliation you could expect were you to vent your anger haughtily and abruptly. You not only will be more effective, the task will be easier as well.

Talking first about your fear can sound something like this:

> I'm afraid to talk with you about something that has made me feel angry.
>> Or,
> I'm afraid that if I tell you what you did that makes me feel angry, you'll get upset and . . . (flunk me, fire me, reject me, tell my friends bad things about me, whatever).
>> Or,
> I need to tell you something, but I'm shaking in my boots.

STEP 3: DESCRIBE THE OFFENSE, HOW IT MADE YOU FEEL, AND WHY

Assume that talking about your fear has disarmed those who have angered you. You've now arrived at the heart of your communication. It's time to construct in your mind *descriptive*, rather than *accusatory* statements. Instead of blaming or striking back at those who offended you, you can describe (1) what they did to violate you, (2) how it made you feel, and (3) why it affected you that way. Rehearse with me these three components of an effective *descriptive* response:

In **Component One,** you describe what they did to make you angry:

> *To your boss:* When you take a commission I earned.
> *To your roommate:* When you leave your dirty
>> dishes for me to wash.
> *To your brother:* When you drive at speeds that
>> scare me.

112

To your friend: When you poke fun at everything
   I say.

In **Component Two, you explain how you feel
about what they did:**

I feel robbed and angry about it.
I feel resentful.
I feel afraid and angry.
I feel put down and furious.

Make an important distinction here: The task is to
describe how you felt about what happened, not how
you felt about those who angered you. So you do not
call them names, blame them, or make accusations.
See the difference:

I feel robbed and angry about it.
   Not,
I feel you're a sneaky s.o.b.

I feel resentful.
   Not,
I feel you are an inconsiderate slob.

I feel afraid and angry.
   Not,
I feel you are a maniac behind the wheel.

I feel put down and furious.
   Not,
I feel you are an inconsiderate, obnoxious,
   patronizing jerk!

In **Component Three,** you describe why you feel the way you do:

> *Because* salespeople deserve to get their commissions.
> *Because* we agreed we'd take care of our own dishes.
> *Because* you unnecessarily risk my getting killed.
> *Because* you make me look stupid.

These are the three components of the *descriptive* statement:

1. What they did. (Their behavior)
2. How you feel. (Your feeling)
3. Why you feel this way. (Your justification for anger)

Here are our four illustrations incorporating the three components:

1. When you take a commission I earned (What your boss did)
   I feel robbed and angry about it (How you feel),
   because salespeople deserve to get their commissions (Why you feel this way).
2. When you leave your dirty dishes for me to wash (What your roommate did)
   I feel resentful (How you feel),
   because we agreed we'd do our own dishes. (Why you feel this way)
3. When you drive at speeds that scare me (What your brother did)

> I feel afraid and angry (How you feel),
> because you unnecessarily risk my getting
> killed. (Why you feel this way)
> 4. When you poke fun at everything I say (What
> your friend did)
> I feel put down and furious (How you feel),
> because you make me look stupid. (Why
> you feel put down, angry)

The purpose of the third component is to check the validity of your anger. When you force yourself to say *because*, you may find your anger is not based on what is true, fair, or realistic, but on something else. You may have been misinformed about or you may have misunderstood something that happened. Perhaps a friend pointed out to others something you're ashamed of and you feel threatened being exposed. Or while you felt slighted by others, you merely imagined they did it. Or maybe your anger is rooted in envy.

Here's a specific illustration. To your teenage daughter whose behavior upset you and who doesn't understand you:

> When you stay out until two A.M. (What she
>   did),
> it makes me afraid and angry (How you feel),
> *because* . . . uh . . . I couldn't stay out that late
>   when I was your age.
> (Why, indeed, you're afraid and angry. But a
>   *valid* reason?)

If you force yourself to say *because*, and you can't discover a defensible reason for your anger, you may save yourself embarrassment. You also can begin to work on any problem within yourself that misdirected you.

On the other hand, if by saying *because* you identify a legitimate reason for your anger, you can express it with more confidence. For example:

> *Because* when you come in so late I can't sleep
>   for worrying about you.
> I keep thinking about the girl down the street
>   who was raped last week.
> (Why you're afraid—and *a good reason* your
>   daughter might understand)

When you identify why you're angry, you can scrutinize whether or not it's valid *before* you let it out. And if you perceive that your anger is unjustified, it will soon lose steam, and what originally infuriated you will seem unimportant after all. As a result, you'll be both true to yourself and avoid harming your important relationships.

In 1970, I came home one evening to find Barbara preparing dinner in tears. Our daughter, a brand-new, typical teenager, had come in from school and thrown on her bedroom floor the dress Barbara had ironed for her that morning. It wasn't the first time. With the hope that I could make her afraid and guilty enough to alter her behavior, I raised my voice and started in: "You're selfish! Your room is a pigpen!" She shouted back, "It's my room!" Then I laid it on a little heavier: "You don't care about your mother! You blah, blah, blah . . ." and she went into her room and slammed the door, which happened whenever I made these kinds of accusations. It was the only way she could take care of herself.

We were only smart enough to know we needed help. So we joined a parenting class that introduced us to the idea of descriptive versus accusatory statements. Instead of bombarding our daughter with negative accusations for throwing her clothes on the floor—which brought the slammed door and cut off communication—I began saying, "Whenever you do that, I get angry because it upsets your mother and we have a terrible dinnertime." She would reply, "They're my clothes and it's my room." And I'd say, "Whenever you defend yourself it frustrates me, because it tells me you want to keep throwing your clothes on the floor." And she'd say, "Mother doesn't have to iron my clothes; I'll do it." And I'd reply, "When you say that, it frustrates me further, because when you throw your clothes on the floor, how can we trust you to iron them?" And so on.

The point is that while the descriptive statements may not have gotten her to take better care of her clothes, rather than having her slam the door and cut me off, we were engaging in communication that had integrity to it.

Your anger exists. In and of itself it's not good or bad; it's not something to glory in or be ashamed of. Your purposes are to control its power creatively so you can be true to yourself and to get those who violate you to stop. Your task is, therefore, neither to suppress it nor to go on a rampage of blaming, but to accept it, to acknowledge, if necessary, any fear of expressing it, and then be direct and descriptive when you let it out. And the point is to practice the three components of the descriptive response until you have them down pat and they're immediately available when your anger flashes.

STEP 4: TELL THOSE WHO MAKE YOU ANGRY WHAT YOU WANT FROM THEM

Here's where you call on your assertiveness skills. Once you've been specific about their offense, your angry feelings, and why you experience them, tell others in positive terms what you want them to do differently, or what you want them to do that is different from what they've been doing.

It may be that the first thing you want them to do is apologize. If so, you can say, "I feel violated by you. I'd like you to apologize for what you did." It cannot be a matter of wanting to humiliate them or make yourself feel powerful. A healthy purpose is to get them to face their failure to respect you and commit themselves to change. You rightly want them to stop abusing you. If they apologize, an immediate thank-you is appropriate. If they don't, it may be because they're overcome with embarrassment or are not particularly articulate. If you sense by their expressions and body language that they regret what they've done and intend to change, you don't need to box them into a strict formula or press them unreasonably—you can let them save face and leave the door open to see how they treat you. Keep in mind that we're talking about people you have to live or work with, or with whom you want to be ongoing friends.

Whether or not they apologize, your main concern now is to tell them directly, in a confident tone of voice, how you want them to treat you in the future:

From now on, I want you to give me the commissions I deserve.

Please do your half of the dishes after this.

I want you to drive within the speed limit whenever I'm with you.

I'd like you to be respectful of me in front of my
friends.

Whenever you ask people to treat you with consideration, you call them to their best without denying
them their freedom. You don't tell them what they
should or must do, but what you would like them to
do. They may not give you what you want, of course,
but it's important to both of you for them to *know* what
you would like from them. Healthy relationships
require that you respect others and expect to be treated
with respect in return.

YOU HAVE A NEW WAY TO EXPRESS ANGER

From now on, when you recognize your anger and
come to the right time and place to express it, you will:

- Direct it to those who violated you, rather than to
others.
- Talk first about your fear, rather than the anger
itself.
- Describe the violation, how it made you feel, and
why.
- Tell others what you want them to do.

And you will be surprised how effective these steps
can be.

SUPPOSE THIS PROCESS
DOESN'T WORK

No matter how respectfully you approach some people, you'll experience various forms of resistance rather than reconciliation. Some of them will withdraw and refuse to apologize or give you signs that they'll honor you in the future. When people do this, they leave your relationship broken and possibly irreparable. If you're dealing with family or friends, this can break your heart. But even if they don't apologize, they may stop treating you disrespectfully, and that, of course, is one of your immediate goals. It also may be the best you can hope for.

Others will not break their relationship with you but may use various tactics to justify their behavior. They may try to excuse themselves by explaining why you shouldn't feel offended: They didn't do what you say they did; you took it the wrong way; they didn't understand what you wanted; they've done the same thing to others who weren't offended; and so on. If their self-defense leaves you uncertain as to their willingness to change their behavior, repeat what you want, stating it again in positive terms:

> I deserve the commission and I want you to
> transfer it to me.
> You suggest you're justified in leaving your
> dishes for me. I disagree, and I ask again,
> please wash them and put them away.
> I don't care about your reasons for driving so fast,
> or how others feel about it; when I'm in the
> car I want you to observe the limit.

You've excused yourself for making fun of me. But
again, I'm asking you to treat me with respect
so we still can be friends.

Some people may become aggressive and try to turn
the tables on you, accusing you of weakness, or of selfishness or of being afraid, as if *you* are the problem. You
can agree that you may *have* or *be* a problem, but if you
want a healthy relationship with them, you must stick
to your insistence that they violated you and you have
a right to have their behavior toward you changed.
You may need to be persistent:

You reviewed that account, but I did the work
on it. I want the commissions that are rightly
mine.
I may not understand your time pressures, but I
have mine too, and we agreed you'd do your
dishes. I want you to respect our agreement.
You're probably right that I'm a baby when it
comes to driving fast, but I still want you to
abide by the law. I'd like you to agree to that.
I'm may be too sensitive and take your ridicule
too seriously, but that's the way I am. And I
want you to be considerate of me.

If you ever handle your anger badly and want to
apologize, do it as soon and as directly as you can. If
you're convinced you were mistreated, however, you
need never disparage your anger by apologizing for it.
The task is to honor your anger in respect for your own
integrity and for the power it has to change how
people treat you.

Of course, when people insist on repeating their

abuse, they rekindle your desire for revenge. They not only show their worst sides, but they also bring out the worst in you. So what can you do when this happens?

To begin, decide you are not going to let revenge seethe in you because you value your own health. With this decision, your desire may immediately go away and you'll feel a great weight lifted from your shoulders. If it doesn't, verbalize your feelings descriptively (go back to the three-component formula) to yourself, and then to the one who's offended you:

When you continue to step on me (What they do)
I feel like getting even with you (How you feel)
because you're refusing to respect me. (Why you feel this way)

You might add, "I don't like this anger in me and want you to stop."

If they insist on continuing their behavior, at the least you can avoid situations that give them opportunity to violate you. It may be as simple as not socializing with your friend or refusing to ride with your brother when he drives (admittedly not easy if he's your primary source of transportation. You may have to weigh the trade-offs). On the other hand, it may take drastic actions such as changing jobs or moving.

When some people find they cannot continue to violate you, they may sever the relationship and disappear. If this happens, there is little you can do, and you'll be better off—an abusive relationship is worse than none at all. In fact, if they continue to violate you, you may have to make the break yourself. If this happens, you can always remain open to the time when they're willing to treat you with respect and renew the relationship.

The point is this: You can only maintain authentic relationships with those who honor your reasonable needs and desires. The offender must acknowledge your pain and respect your insistence that the abusive behavior cease. As noted, some people have trouble relating at such a level. Your repeated descriptive directness may break their resistance. If it doesn't, at least you'll know you've done your best, and you'll have been true both to them and your own best interests.

DEALING WITH UNFINISHED BUSINESS

What if you're holding a grudge toward people who have died, moved far away, or simply are out of your life? Perhaps a parent or sibling abused you when you were a child, or a friend betrayed or attacked you, and you never responded to their actions. Now they're gone. How do you resolve this unfinished business?

To have suffered such violence was tragic. But to cling to your anger is worthless and needless and magnifies the tragedy. If you see this and want to free yourself from it, here are several things you can do:

VENT YOUR ANGER IN HARMLESS WAYS

You may want to hit a pillow while shouting and swearing in an empty room. Or you might dictate a letter into a tape recorder describing what the person did, how it made you feel, and why you're still angry: "You made me look like a fool to all my friends!" Our strong feelings beg to be expressed. This yearning is a primal psychological or emotional reality, perhaps even a spiritual one. Some compare it to the deep railings against God and the long lamentations of the ancient prophets and psalmists. And many people say they're helped by venting this way.

FORGIVE THOSE WHO VIOLATED YOU AND ARE NOW GONE FROM YOUR LIFE

Blowing off steam like I've just described may make you feel good temporarily. That's because you release the negative pressure. But the grudge may not go away because you haven't dealt with your abiding attitude, your rancor. Forgiving those who offend will do that for you. But where do we get the will and strength to forgive them?

We may find it easy to forgive if we're sick to death of carrying the grudge and are ready to do anything to get rid of it. We also may be more readily able to express forgiveness if we

- Clearly see that all people can be selfish, mean, and irrationally abusive—including nice people like you and me.
- Keep in mind that we violate others and need forgiveness ourselves.
- Are convinced that buried resentments erode our own well-being, that they hurt *us* rather than the people against whom we hold them.

But what if we can't stand the thought of forgiving them? Suppose our resentments control us? What do we do? Fortunately, we can work on it. And it's never too late to begin.

One thing you can do is acknowledge to yourself that you don't want to let go of your grudge. Simply facing the fact you are resisting forgiveness can liberate you to let go of it. Be honest with yourself about your wanting to hold on to your grudge, and that act of honesty can, paradoxically, trigger the willingness to do it. So you might say to yourself, He doesn't deserve to be forgiven for deliberately making me look like a fool to my friends. I don't want to let him off the hook. I want to hold on to my resentment, even if it kills me. I am not going to forgive him. And then see what happens.

To forgive is of critical importance to a future worth living. It's the only way we can free ourselves from the pain we were caused and the burden of carrying the debilitating grudge. It can generate peace within us like nothing else. Stop for a moment and let the negative feelings that go with your grudge come to the surface. Then choose whether you want to continue carrying them: I do or I don't. If you don't, forgive those who offended you and compare your new set of emotions with those generated by your long-suppressed anger.

TRY A FORGIVENESS CONVERSATION

If you find yourself wanting to forgive but don't seem able to do it, you may want to try an imaginary talk with the offenders. Imagine that those who violated you but who are now gone are actually present, and that you're talking with them. By visualizing them in your mind's eye, you can make your forgiveness vivid and memorable, thus giving it increased emotional power. Once you've set the scene and can *see* yourself in their presence, you can say something like, "I've held a grudge against you for making me look foolish to my friends and I'm tired of it. I forgive you for how you treated me, and I ask you to forgive my shortcomings and offenses. I regret I didn't say these things when we were together, but I want to say them now. I don't want to live with this between us."

Let them accept your apology and forgiveness. Then feel what it's like to witness yourself giving them a long, warm embrace.

Symbolize Forgiveness and Let Go of Your Grudge

Some who find that the imaginary conversation doesn't work turn to an exercise like this: Write down what they did, how it made you feel, and why (the three-component formula), and how you understand their action as an offense. Top it off with a direct statement of forgiveness (something like the above). Then burn the paper in the sink and wash the ashes down the drain. Let this little ceremony symbolize your willingness to let go of your grudge and have it washed away. If necessary, do this weekly, even daily, until either your pain fades or you're convinced the ritual isn't going to work.

A similar ceremony: Instead of burning the paper, bury it in your yard (or flower box). Let it represent your commitment to *bury your grudge outside of your heart and let your forgiveness bring an end to it.* Mark your calendar for when you'll dig it up, perhaps in a week or a month. If your resentment doesn't disappear by the time you exhume the paper, write another statement and hold another burial ceremony.

If you find that your willingness to forgive, imaginary monologues, and ceremonies don't get you past your grudge, you might tell your story to an empathic friend, a support group, or, if necessary, a competent counselor. For some people, talking rather than writing brings clarity and courage, and this form of expression offers the advantage of support and insight from different perspectives.

Choosing how to process immediate or longtime anger requires thought and energy, and the steps may be difficult and prove awkward at first. Indeed, we usually do not stop lifelong habits easily. But with a little reflection, patience, and practice, you'll soon create positive habits based on more than good intentions. And when you do, you'll feel infinitely more real, you'll be able to congratulate yourself for all your growth, and you'll enjoy yourself more.

And you'll still be a *nice person.*

Mistake #5

REASONING WITH IRRATIONALITY

You refer to a friend in local politics as a compromiser. You mean that he works well with others. A mutual acquaintance overhears that part of your remarks and thinks you mean he has no backbone. The next day she tells your friend and he is upset. When you hear about it, you call him to explain. And as you begin, your mature, reasonable old friend blows his stack, calls you a liar, and slams down the phone.

A few years back, I drove to our busy village to do bank business and pick up some nails and brackets at the hardware store. Just as I spotted a convenient parking space, I noticed that the old Chevy ahead of me had stopped and might be going to back into it. So I kept my distance and waited. And waited. Cars soon piled up behind me and at least one driver blew his horn. I was getting impatient, too, when an elderly woman, with some difficulty, made her way slowly out of the front right door, and I concluded that she was being dropped off for shopping. So I slid headfirst into the parking space, counting myself lucky.

As I walked to the curb, the Chevy's backup lights went on, and I could see that the little old man who was driving and who had enough trouble with parking was now flustered to realize he didn't have a spot. I didn't feel guilty for taking the space I thought he didn't want, but I immediately felt sorry for him, and took a few steps back toward my car. At the same time, he continued to sit there, and the cars in back of him began beeping mercilessly and attracting attention. As he finally drove off, a young man suddenly put himself in my face and said loudly enough for everyone on the block to hear, "I saw what you just did to that old man and I think it was shitty!" I was stunned and tried to give him the whole picture, but he stalked off ranting to passersby—some of whom knew me—that he'd never seen anything more inconsiderate. I ran after him, still wanting to explain myself, but he shouted, **"Shut up and don't talk to me!"** His attack left me feeling terrible, upset, and—shitty. And it took me a long time to get rid of that feeling.

Life does not always accord with reason. Dimensions of our experiences are utterly illogical. Some of these dimensions are positive—think of romance, passion, adventure, wonder, and serendipitous, crazy things. They give color to our lives. But some irrationalities are disturbing, especially people's negative, emotional reactions to us that have no basis in reality. More specifically, I'm talking about criticism and personal attacks on us for things we didn't do or, at least, didn't mean to do, or were actually justified in doing.

Whenever people think we've violated or threatened them, one internal voice tells them immediately to flee conflict at any cost. And that impulse is strong. But in some cases—those with which we're concerned here—the equally immediate voice of anger, with its interest in retaliation, drowns out that voice and, rather than taking flight, they attack us. A co-worker flies off the handle over how you treat her, even though you relate to everyone at the office in the same respectful way. A friend spreads the word that you did something with sinister or selfish motives, when the truth is you acted aboveboard and without a trace of selfishness. You accidentally step on the toes of a family member and he explodes as if you did it on purpose.

We cannot predict when people will irrationally attack us or what form it will take. Their anger may flash and quickly wane, leaving them sullen and withdrawn, or they may drag out a federal case against us. They may talk to others about us or pick a face-to-face fight. They may rave like proverbial loose cannons, their exploding emotions and blind impulses ricocheting off the walls of our encounter, or they may simply seethe and stab us in the back when no one's looking. No matter what their style, when people irrationally attack us, we feel they have impugned our character and name, threatening our reputation.

Such attacks, whatever their form, leave us hurt, shaken, frightened, and exasperated. Of course, as nice people, we do not retaliate by unleashing our anger on our accusers. We may blow off to others in hope of gaining their support, but with those who accost us we control our responses and, with all good intentions, try to explain what *really* happened.

To be sure, we have our reasons for being reasonable. We want our calm logic both to settle our attackers down and to straighten them out. They offer us a barrage of reasons to justify their attack, so we want them to see the good reasons why they are *not* justified. At the same time, as illogical as people seem to us at such times, our niceness insists that we give them the benefit of the doubt and treat them as if they're mature, rather than challenge their motives or assume there is something wrong with their mental makeup. And then we hope that by winning our case rationally we will confirm our own sanity to ourselves and establish an acceptable basis for our behavior in the future.

Making a rational defense in such situations is our mistake. But because it is the perfect extension of our niceness and seems like the right thing to do, it's hard for us to see it as a mistake. So before we go further, look at why it is.

REASONS WHY REASONING IS A MISTAKE

RESPONDING TO IRRATIONALITY WITH RATIONALITY DOESN'T WORK

Reasoning doesn't take seriously the gap between actual events and the irrationality of those who attack us. We respond based on erroneous assumptions. We believe that if we set the record straight, our attackers will suddenly understand and rescind their charges. We think that if we're reasonable, they'll be reasonable, that if we explain why we did what we did and they still have differences with us, they'll be happy to agree to disagree. It's akin to reasoning with a child who is throwing a tantrum. We make a basic miscalculation: We see them not as they are but as we would like them to be, namely, rational. Defending ourselves this way works about as well as trying to catch the ocean in a net.

OUR ATTACKERS AREN'T INTERESTED IN HEARING US DEFEND OURSELVES

Their immediate needs are to know that we hear them, we appreciate their hurt, and we see that they have a right to be upset. When we defend ourselves, we ignore these needs, and they know it. They want certain things from us, and we offer them something they don't want to hear. We're not on their wavelength.

REASONING IS A FORM OF SUPPRESSING OUR ANGER

We're angry and they know it; if we accosted them as they have us, they know they'd be irritated, if not enraged. Yet because we are nice, we blithely act as if we're not angry and calmly try to defend ourselves. So both our anger and the conflict get buried and go unresolved.

Even more of a problem, our well-meaning, rational responses not only fail to resolve the conflict, they also tend to make the conflict worse and the damage greater. Irritated by our defensive discourse, our accusers rearm their charges, striking back more vigorously. The realization that our efforts aren't working makes us try harder to overpower them with more rationality, creating a still larger gap between us. If the distance and damage become too much and we feel we've failed, we write them off and perhaps even sever the relationship.

A DIFFERENT RESPONSE TO IRRATIONALITY

Are you convinced that reasoning in response to irrational attacks is not productive? Would you like an effective alternative way to respond? If so, the first step, even before you know what to put in its place, is to decide you'll no longer defend yourself. Then memorize or post a statement like one of these:

> To reason with irrationality does more harm
>   than good, so from now on I will not do it.
> If I defend myself, I will make matters worse, so
>   I'm not going to do it anymore.

Assume you've taken this step. You now need to learn how to respond to negative irrationality in ways that not only leave your integrity intact but that also repair your relationships. Begin with a commitment to understand these attacks and how your responses need to be shaped.

Look first at five things we know about these attacks.

1. People will attack you for a variety of reasons. They may

- Wrongly interpret something you do as harmful or threatening.
- Be suffering a temporary physical or emotional crisis (heart attack, loss of job, divorce, etc.) that distorts their perceptions of reality.
- Disagree so much with your expressed opinions on sex, politics, or religion that they can't think straight or control their feelings.
- Find you in the way of their interests: You are the wrong person innocently in the wrong spot at the wrong time.
- Be upset by the news you bring to them.
- Transfer to you feelings of guilt or anger that you trigger in them.
- Feel bad about themselves but cannot blame themselves.
- Desperately want something from you that you won't or can't give them.
- Think you hold power over them, and you tap their fears about their own inadequacies.
- Want to control you and you refuse to let them do that.
- Idealize you and you disappoint their unrealistic expectations.
- Prejudge you for your race, gender, sexual orientation, physical features, or anything else for which you shouldn't be judged.
- Take medications that make them confused and irritable.
- Be mentally ill, substance abusers, or damaged victims of domestic violence who are chronically angry, and they're acting out.

2. Identifying the causes of the attack can help you respond more creatively. Irrational attacks more often than not emerge from a combination of sources. Thus pinning down the causes is not always easy. But it's important, because various causes call for different responses. For example, an attack that springs from a simple misunderstanding requires a different response than one that arises from mental illness. Also, when you know what's behind a strong emotional reaction, it's rendered less disturbing and easier to handle. Whenever you're attacked, therefore, immediate questions to ask yourself are, Why is this happening? What's going on here that doesn't meet the eye?

3. Although your accusers' indictments strike you as absurd, they make sense to them. Unfortunately, you usually are dealing with a double dysfunction: (1) irrational attacks and (2) the attackers' convictions that they're being perfectly rational. Once you understand this, you can relate to them with patience and, potentially, with more effectiveness. It is especially important to be sensitive to this when you're dealing with friends you don't want to lose.

4. Your accusers feel hurt and are out of control. To see this may help you not to take the attack personally and overreact yourself. What you did may have triggered the attack, but it is their hurt, fear, and emotional upset that caused it, not you. To realize this is important because you don't want to give their irrationality any more stature or power than it deserves. And the last thing you want to do is exacerbate their highly charged reactions, which, if not aggravated, like all anger will tend to subside rather quickly.

I'm not suggesting you condone dysfunctional behavior or let bullies walk on you. I'm simply concerned that you focus first on their hurt and upset. Whether you violated them or not, they have reacted negatively and you must take their reaction seriously. Here's the point: Their feelings of hurt and emotional upset are not the same as the irrational charge they level at you. And because the hurt and upset precede the charge, you need to respond to the feelings *before* you handle the charge itself.

5. You are engaging in a dynamic process in which sensitivity, timing, and flexibility are important. The process requires you at every moment to identify your feelings and decide how to express them. It also calls you to gauge the momentary changes in your assailants' emotional states created by your responses. In addition, it means discerning what your assailants can handle from you at any given time, and then determining when to speak up and when to back off.

A CAUTION

Early on, double-check your conclusion that your accusers are irrational. These attacks throw you for a loop, threatening your personal interests, which you feel the need to protect. So it's possible you've overreacted and are wrong about the assumed irrationality. You are convinced that they've drawn conclusions that don't compute. But if you check your judgment before confronting them, it may save you both embarrassment and an important relationship.

If those who attacked you seem to get control of themselves and you think it's a simple case of misunderstanding, you may be able to test quickly what is happening. You might say, "I'm sorry, I think I've confused you. May we talk about it?" Or "I need to get something straight. Did you realize I meant such-and-such?" You'll learn very quickly whether it's more than a mere misunderstanding. If the response is "Oh, *that's* what you meant? I thought you were talking about so-and-so," it may get resolved right then. But if irrationality is in charge, you'll get further fireworks, and no amount of carefully crafted explanations will save you.

Look for other signs: Do your accusers have a history of acting this way? Do they show complete disinterest in your side of the story? Are they unwilling to agree to disagree or are they only interested in seeing you discredited and punished? After the attack, do they want to act as if nothing has happened? Might they be on medications that produce irritable behavior? Do people whose objectivity you respect draw the same conclusions you do? If you answer *yes* to any of these questions, you're probably dealing with an irrational attack.

Still, you may be wrong. Perhaps you can ask third parties to hear both sides of the story and give their evaluation. If they conclude that your accuser has a right to be upset with you, and you see their point, you can apologize and repair your relationship. On the other hand, if they confirm your judgment that you have been wrongly accused, you can proceed to the dialogue more confidently.

INITIATING AN ALTERNATIVE PROCESS

Because you now have a new understanding of irrational attacks, you'll no longer immediately feel obligated to defend yourself. But that's not enough. You must learn to respond in ways that transform what has happened so that the truth is not only honored, but your relationship is also repaired. Look at a scenario in which a young woman, a nice person, responds rationally to a personal attack.

Mary serves as secretary for a service club that is reorganizing. One of her tasks is to inform members, on behalf of the steering committee, about their committee assignments. One morning she receives a phone call from a member whom everyone respects as an engineer, but who also is known as someone difficult to work with. He tells her he is angry at her memo assigning him to the facilities committee. He had made it clear he wants to work on the budget committee and insists that she transfer him.

She immediately recalls when the steering committee agreed that, in spite of his preference, they wanted his expertise on facilities. So she begins to explain why he was placed where he was. He interrupts, saying he resents their disregard for his wishes. Wanting to be helpful, Mary begins to explain how he might appeal the board's decision. He tells her he is sick and tired of the whole damned process and, raising his voice, says, **"Just change the assignment!"**

Mary calmly begins to spell out why she cannot do that as the secretary. He cuts her off and shouts, **"Put me on the budget committee!"** She repeats that she doesn't have that authority and begins to explain how easy it'll be for him to get it changed. He now starts screaming about how everyone is controlling him, including Mary, which surprises and confuses her. Before she can catch her breath, he swears and slams down the phone. Mary feels violated, bewildered, angry, and exasperated. And she has a problem on her hands.

Now, put yourself in Mary's place. Imagine it is you who receives that devastating phone call. Keep in mind the five understandings we've just looked at:

1. Irrational attacks may spring from a single source or from many.
2. Identifying the irrationality's source helps you respond more effectively.
3. Those who attack you believe they are being rational.
4. Something hurtful and upsetting in them causes the attacks, not something in you.
5. Sensitivity, timing, and flexibility are important.

Confirm in your own mind that his attack is undeserved and harmful to you, to him, and to your club. Assume that your primary goal is to create a mutually respectful, functional relationship with him. Now follow me through several steps toward your goal down a different path than the rational one that Mary tried.

STEP 1: CALL TIME OUT TO CALM DOWN

Your primary purpose is not to control your attacker or defend yourself, but to control your reaction to his irrational attack. He may be out of control, but you also are upset, angry, and, perhaps, in shock. So you can say to yourself, Cool it! You can let him unload lightning and thunder, and when the storm has blown over, you'll be calmer and have a more placid atmosphere in which to respond. You will not want to be silent about your feelings forever, of course, and you don't want him to rant on and on. But you realize that it's more important to resolve a conflict effectively than immediately, and that time is on your side. So you can calm yourself down, hear him out briefly, and, when he gives you the chance to speak, acknowledge that he caught you by surprise and ask for a moment to recover.

If he is unwilling to hear you and continues to rail, you might follow with, "I want to hear you, but I need you to slow down." If he goes on ranting, when he takes a breath, you can step in and say, "Let me see if I understand what you said," and then paraphrase what you heard. If he will not let you do this, or is abusive, you can say, "I don't like to be spoken to like this; I'm going to ask you to stop." If he is so out of control he is unable to stop, you may want to back off and ask him to let you call him back. Your main purpose at the moment is to defuse the volatile atmosphere and get control of yourself. (If you're attacked by letter or hear of accusations secondhand, you'll likely have plenty of time to calm yourself.)

STEP 2: GENERATE EMPATHY FOR YOUR ATTACKER

To have empathy is to be sensitive to his feelings, which as a nice person may come naturally to you. But to empathize is not to take responsibility for him or try to solve his problems. Neither does it mean you feel sorry for him, express pity on his behalf, or, as sympathy does, agree with his feelings: Empathy and sympathy are entirely different responses.

Empathy involves an escalating set of responses through which you move from one level to another as if ascending a flight of stairs, progressively positioning yourself to relate to your attacker more closely and more effectively.

See Things from His Perspective

At a first level, empathy merely requires you to see things from his perspective. Once you have control of your emotional reaction, to use your imagination to stand in his place wearing his shoes, as it were, trying to see things through his eyes, if at all possible. It's a first step of understanding.

Find Compassion

At a second level, empathy is to have compassion for him. Compassion means "to suffer with." It's now a matter of seeing him as a hurting human being who because of this encounter is now a part of you, a person who lives inside you. It is to respect and care enough about him to suffer with him in his pain.

Of course you may not be eager to experience his pain. He attacked you. And you immediately wanted to attack him back, to rail at him with blame. You couldn't do that, of course, because you're a nice person and this relationship is important to you; you want it to work, and you know that blaming—while it would make you feel justified for the moment—would do nothing to warm his spirit or improve his behavior.

Indeed, it would make him more defensive. So you have said no to your own powerful emotions and calmed yourself down. You now can take advantage of instincts that are fine-tuned to care for those who are hurting and muster all the maturity, skill, and compassion of which you're capable in order to feel his pain. Again, you are not asked by empathy to approve his reaction or to let him walk all over you. It's merely a matter of being willing to understand and feel the frightening power of the pain he feels.

To find compassion, you will have to listen carefully for the words he uses and, more important, pay attention to the feelings behind his words. You often can discern them in the tone, volume, and emotional content of his voice. (Were he present, you also could observe his facial expressions and body language.) And this may not be easy. Even as you are trying to discern what he's feeling, the clamor of voices within you will be calling you to formulate your rebuttal—it may take hard work not to let them distract you from learning exactly who he is at the moment.

Reflect His Feelings Back to Him

At the third level of empathy, you can reflect his feelings back to him. If you are able to calm your own anger, listen to his story, avoid defensiveness, and identify with his pain, you then can **feed back to him your awareness of his upset.** By so doing, you will disarm much of his anger because he will see that you take him seriously and believe he is worth your time and concern.

It's important at this point to distinguish between

reflecting people's feelings and *repeating their words*. As I've noted, it's sometimes necessary to recap what others are saying to make sure you've heard them correctly and get them to listen to you. But here the task is not to restate words; it's to reflect, as if you are a human mirror, the strong feelings that propel their attacks.

If you simply were to reflect the words of the fellow in our illustration and he said, "You've treated me badly!" you would follow with, "I hear you saying I've treated you badly!" If he said, "I insist that I be assigned to the budget committee," you would respond, "You insist on assignment to the budget committee."

But this is not empathy. It's a word game that leads nowhere, and it may make him more irritable and resistant. On the other hand, if you reflect his feelings, he will feel heard and appreciated and he will more than likely be receptive to what you have to say. Empathy at this level sounds like:

> You are **angry** (the feeling) at the way I've treated you.
> **Not,**
> You say I've treated you badly.

> You **resent** (the feeling) not being on the budget committee.
> **Not,**
> I hear you saying you want to be on the budget committee.

One way to reflect feelings, particularly when you are new to the practice, is to begin your response with the words, *You feel angry . . . upset . . . frustrated . . . hurt*—whatever the feeling. You don't want to begin every sentence this way, but if you cement this phrase in your mind it'll keep you focused on what you're trying to do.

If you read and mirror his resentment correctly, he may say, "You *bet* I resent it!" If so, you'll have let him know that you understand him and give him permission to express his feelings further in a context of acceptance. If he denies being angry or is slow to catch your drift, you simply may want to say, "I've heard you and I understand."

Validate His Feelings

At the fourth level of empathy you validate your attacker's feelings by accepting his experience. Again, this doesn't mean you agree with him. Nor does it ask you to tell him, "I know exactly how you feel" (even if you do—and you probably don't). And it certainly doesn't mean that you apologize to him—an apology fits when you have actually violated someone, which is not the case here. To validate his feelings is simply to accept his experience as both real and legitimate and to tell him so. It involves saying things like:

> It must have been hard to have been put on the facilities committee with no explanation. No wonder you were upset.
> You wanted to be on the budget committee. I can understand why you're resentful.
> If I saw it the way you do, I think I'd be angry too.
> I'm sure I can't appreciate what you are going through.

Note the difference between empathy and the inappropriate apology: "We were *wrong* to place you on the facilities committee." And see how it differs also from a rational and moralistic defense: "You were put on the facilities committee because of your expertise, and you shouldn't be angry with us."

Those who study the helping professions generally agree that empathy is 90 percent of what it takes to disarm and repair relationships with those who are hurt and upset. We long have expected empathy from counselors, social workers, nurses and doctors, clergy, and teachers. With the popularization of psychology since the fifties—just about everybody now knows what ego trips and paranoia are—the conviction has spread that just about everyone who wants to can develop the skills required for empathy.

If you can early on (1) identify your attacker's feelings, (2) feel compassionately with his upset and pain, (3) reflect back to him what you sense, and (4) validate his feelings by accepting his experience, you will relieve a good bit of his emotional overload. Relating to him will be easier, and it just might effect immediate reconciliation. If it doesn't, it at least should gain you his trust so that in time you can productively discuss which committee he will join. Of course, empathy alone is not going to make him happy with an assignment to the facilities committee. But because it involves respecting his freedom, empathy can evoke positive responses from him and go so much further to resolve the conflict than efforts to defend your position rationally.

Step 3: Express Sorrow about His Pain

This step takes you beyond merely identifying, reflecting, and validating your attacker's feelings. It lets him know you also feel bad about what caused him to feel as he did: "You've been hurt because you've felt mistreated. I'm sorry about this." Here again, you're not saying that you wronged him or that his attack was justified. You're letting him know he's appreciated and he's been heard, two of his main concerns at the moment. And if you do this, you can move closer to the moment when he will perceive and treat you differently.

If he wrongly misinterprets your empathy and sorrow as agreement, or as an apology and, wanting you to see things his way, will not listen to your attempts to clarify what you mean, you can say something like "You act as if I agreed with you. This frustrates me. I feel bad about what you experienced, but if we're going to work with each other, I must have your commitment to respect my intentions."

Assume you've taken the first three steps: (1) You called time out; (2) you worked through the levels of empathy; and (3) you expressed sorrow over causing him pain. You have laid the foundation for mutual respect and a measure of civil conversation. It's even possible you have freed him to come to his senses and apologize. It's also possible you haven't. If that's the case, resolution and reconciliation become more difficult. So these next four steps are more complex and precarious, and they require more finely honed skills—you may need to review this section and rehearse or role-play the first three skills before moving on.

STEP 4: ASK HIM TO ENGAGE IN AN ONGOING EXCHANGE OF FEELINGS

At some point, once you sense that he's calmed down and a measure of trust and respect has been reached, you can broach the subject of his unfair accusations that made you angry. Getting to this point may take time, and you may not want to do it in this conversation. Sooner or later, however, if you're ever to effect a satisfying resolution that will form the basis of a healthy working relationship, it will be important to express the negative side of your experience with him.

You can offer to go first. If you feel it's important for him to know both your position and how you feel about the conflict, say so directly. If you believe that two-way civil discourse is important to a resolution, tell him. You might suggest that you listen to each other without interrupting. If he agrees, when you finish telling him how you feel, invite him to tell you how he feels about what you said. Your purpose is to build a pattern of listening so that you can understand each other emotionally as well as each other's positions.

Taking this step when both of you are calm is critical. Thus you'll need to know what's going on in each of you. Is he still on a rampage? Has the storm inside *you* passed? Is your throat tight or has it relaxed? Listen to your body; it can tell you whether you're free from being dominated by fear, resentment, rage, disorientation, or frustration. Once you discern that both of you are relatively calm and focused, tell him, directly and vulnerably, what's going in you:

> I felt violated by your attack, whether you
> > intended it or not. Your anger made me tense.
> > I don't know how to talk about it.

You'll have to be patient with me. I've been
upset by your charge that I'm controlling you,
and I don't know what to say.
I'm having trouble handling my confusion and
resentment. You attacked me and that made
me angry at you.

The pattern runs like this: Tell him what you feel, listen
for his feelings in return, then reflect them back to him.
When he responds again, tell him once more what you
are feeling, and listen to him again. If you keep the focus
on being open about your feelings, you have a better
chance, in time, of resolving both of your concerns.

At any time he may try to change the subject to avoid
facing what he's done. Ask him to stay with the subject
and stick to the facts. Once you've achieved some clarity
on each other's feelings, suggest that you take a break to
reflect on what you've heard and absorb the experience.
You may want to set a time when you'll talk again.

STEP 5: REQUEST A FAIR HEARING OF YOUR STORY

You listened with respect to his case against you. Along
with knowing how you're feeling, he needs to hear
and understand your position as you do his. When you
think he's ready to be reasonable, you might look him
in the eyes and say, "My side of the story is important
to me. I'd like you to listen to it."

If he signals he's willing, you can begin to explain
the committee's decision-making process, its authority
and yours, its rationale for assigning him to the facilities committee, and the process for appealing his

assignment. If he's not willing to listen to you, you can tell him it leaves you at a loss. You might say, "I respect your need and right to be heard. But I also need you to appreciate me and my side of the story."

STEP 6: IF HE CANNOT RESPOND POSITIVELY, PERHAPS YOU CAN CREATE A CLIMATE FOR AGREEING TO DISAGREE

Wanting to tell your side of the story may trigger a repeat of his original reaction. If it does, you can call time out again, be empathic once more, and work again to clarify feelings. This may be all you can do until he becomes reasonable, which may be never. You can continue to seek understanding, however, under the assumption that both of you want to resolve your differences and, barring that, will be willing to accept them.

If he shows signs of being reasonable but still disagrees, remind yourself that your goal is a relationship based not on agreement, but on your concern for understanding, for mutual respect and honesty. So when the dust settles and you find you still disagree, you might offer, "It's obvious we see this very differently. No wonder we have conflict. This may take work by both of us."

When you say this to him directly and calmly, you communicate the idea that disagreements are normal, and that it is helpful to have different opinions expressed and accepted. It's possible that no one has ever talked to him like this when he's acted this way before. Your casual candor may ease any tension that remains, enabling him to reflect a bit more on himself, see the unreasonableness of his position, and make a turnabout. And, of course, it may not.

If it doesn't, and he escalates the stormy atmosphere, and you don't know what to do, you can ask him once again for time out to get your bearings: "Please be patient with me. I don't know what to say. I'll get back to you."

Because you're dealing with non- or irrationality, it's important to realize that all your time-outs, all your empathy, all your exchange of feelings, all your requests for patience, all your desire to resolve the conflict, all your understanding and objectivity, may accomplish little or nothing.

So what if you end up feeling mistreated and frustrated? You may conclude that at the least he owes you an apology. If so, when the right moment comes, you can tell him: "I think you treated me badly and owe me an apology." If he's able to say, "Yes, I was wrong and unreasonable, I'm sorry," you can say, "Thank you," and extend your hand to him. (In more personal relationships such a moment may lead to tears and embraces.) Your relationship may have all the repair it needs.

If he still wants to act as if he's done nothing abusive and will not apologize, there is little you can do. A forced apology has no meaning. He may even reject the idea that he helped create the conflict. In fact, he may put all the blame on you, insisting that you as well as the committee owe *him* an apology.

If so, you'll need to decide what you're willing and not willing to do to maintain a working relationship. You can tell him once more that you're sorry he felt mistreated and that you'll try not to upset him again, but you do not do well to pretend everything is all right. In the end, having leveled with him, even if you can't create something functional or get him to agree to disagree—which would be sad—at least you'll know you've been true both to yourself and him.

STEP 7: LET HIM KNOW YOU WILL NOT TOLERATE BEING ATTACKED

Even if you don't receive an apology, you can maintain the integrity of your relationship if you use the three-component formula of the last chapter to express your anger:

> When you shout and swear at me (What he did)
> I feel abused (How you felt)
> because I did not intentionally violate you and I
> listened respectfully to your side of the story.
> (Why you felt abused)

If he ignores you, continues his tantrum, and attacks you again, ask him politely to stop. If he won't do it, you either can sit there and let him berate you or you can break further communication with him. To make such a break shows respect for yourself. And to be respectful of him when you make it, tell him directly what you are doing and invite him to reestablish your relationship whenever he's willing not to abuse you.

NEW WAYS TO RESPOND TO IRRATIONAL ATTACKS

When wrongly assaulted, you now can take the following steps, skipping or repeating some of them or rearranging their order as the dialogue requires:

- Call time out to gain equilibrium and composure.
- Express empathy with your accusers' predicaments and feelings.

- Let them know you're sorry they feel hurt and are upset.
- Encourage the mutual exchange of feelings.
- If they become respectful, ask them to hear your side of the story.
- If necessary, in the end, ask them to agree to disagree.
- Let them know you'll not tolerate being abused.

You no doubt will encounter irrational attacks in the future as you have in the past. From now on, you will not have to offer rational explanations in response to them. Neither will you need to ignore, condone, or cower under them. Each time you can decide how much energy and time the relationship is worth. Depending on your decision, and always responding to your accusers with respect, you then can employ as few or as many of these steps as necessary to heal your relationship.

Your efforts, successful or not, will make you feel good about yourself. On occasion, in the heat of the encounter, you'll no doubt blow your cool, say the wrong thing, or fail to say all sorts of things you later wish you had. Even so, now knowing better and having made the effort, you'll find your new way of responding so much more satisfying and effective than trying to defend yourself rationally.

And you'll still be a *nice person.*

Mistake #6
TELLING LITTLE LIES

The boss suddenly assigns you a new partner. You each go about your separate business in the morning, but every afternoon, hour after hour, you have to sit side by side with him to review financial reports. Your offices are not air-conditioned, he sweats something terrible, and his body odor knocks you over. He's a good guy who works hard and you don't want to hurt his feelings. After a few days he tells you how much he appreciates working with you.

Not long after we were married, Barbara and I met a nice couple at a party and they immediately invited us to dinner at their home. On the appointed evening, as we devoured delicious appetizers, the husband mentioned that his wife had prepared an old family recipe of mashed potatoes topped with a special cheddar

153

cheese. When the meal was served, my potatoes were lumpy, tepid, and tasteless. As we cleared the table for dessert, the hostess looked at me and asked, "By the way, how did you like the potatoes?" I told her a lie.

We nice people don't lie to exploit others or to satisfy our own selfish ends. Any of us under threatening circumstances will tell a lie to promote the common good or save someone we love—like prisoners during war lie to their captors. You probably will lie to people who are being pushy about something that's none of their business. More than likely you will shade the truth to avoid conflict with those who are important to you. And certainly at times you will lie, you say, to spare the feelings of other nice people.

More specifically, you tell lies whenever you believe you cannot *tell the truth and be nice at the same time*. We call these predicaments dilemmas, that is, social situations that offer us two choices, each of which appears to be equally bad. In these kinds of dilemmas, both choices—*nice but not honest* and *honest but not nice*—seem intolerable. But when you are trapped and don't know how to escape, as a nice person, you choose to lie.

Two realities create these nice-or-truthful dilemmas. First, they happen when people fail to fulfill their commitments to us or don't measure up to our reasonable expectations. A member of your volunteer committee, though a very nice person, isn't doing her part, and the others are upset. A co-worker's lack of personal hygiene is driving you crazy. A friend house-sits for you while you vacation, and when you return your plants are dead and the cat is famished. In these cases, we tend to lie by saying nothing and by pretending everything's all right.

Second, these dilemmas arise when others expect responses from us that don't reflect our true feelings or opinions. For your birthday, your sister gives you colored hankies you dislike and don't need, and expects you to say, "What a wonderful present!" A member of your tennis club asks to be your doubles partner and, although you like her, she can't keep up with your game. Your neighbor paints his stucco house an obnoxious color he's ecstatic about and asks what you think of it. Your niece sings badly at her recital and waits with bated breath for your bouquets. A colleague proudly shows you a portrait of his six-month-old, and the kid is the homeliest baby you've ever seen. In cases like these, which we face almost every day, we lie by keeping a straight face and by telling people exactly what they long to hear.

THREE WAYS TO HANDLE THE TRUTH

People in these dilemmas usually choose one of three ways to treat the truth. Look at the story of the lumpy, tepid, tasteless mashed potatoes.

OPTION 1: EVADE THE TRUTH

Here I would have tried to weasel out of the dilemma by changing the subject or by using noncommittal words.

SHE: By the way, how did you like the potatoes?

I: The meal was fine, thanks. And the asparagus was fantastic!

SHE: Oh . . . good! But [insensitively] I meant, How were the *potatoes*?

I: Uh, well, I, they . . . they were . . . *interesting*. Special! Unique! Yes, that's it; I don't think I've ever had potatoes like these before.

SHE: (*Continuing to be insensitive*): I don't mean to put you on the spot, but I was wondering how you *liked* them.

Of course, her insensitivity did put me on the spot. I tried to skirt the truth, and she tried to stop me. In one sense, she was right, for even if this option lets us off the hook for a moment—or forever—it always fails: The truth is excused from our relationships, our integrity is lost, the dilemma remains unsatisfied.

OPTION 2: TELL THE TRUTH BLUNTLY

In this dialogue, I would describe exactly what I thought of them.

SHE: By the way, how did you like the potatoes?

I: Well, to tell the truth, the potatoes were lumpy, tepid, and tasteless. Even the melted cheddar couldn't save them. I thought they were terrible, probably the worst mashed potatoes I've ever tried to eat.

In any given dilemma, if we think we can get away with it, we nice people may try to evade telling the truth. But we **never** choose this option. We were taught that this kind of truth-telling hurts people, and we work hard not to do that. Nasty people may talk this way, but to us, even the thought of telling hard truths so bluntly is unacceptable; it goes against the grain of everything we want to be or have people think about us.

Of course we all know that on certain important occasions the most caring thing to do is to deliver the telling blow of truth because nothing short of such a blow will serve. And there are times when lies will have such drastic consequences that they force us to be honest. But in this story of the potatoes, considering the newness of our relationship and the little that was at stake, this criterion doesn't apply. So, as a nice person, I immediately turn to what I think is our only viable choice.

OPTION 3: SET THE HARD TRUTH ASIDE

In this case, I would—as I did—tell what we nice people call a little white lie, even when it's a bold-faced whopper.

> SHE: By the way, how did you like the potatoes?
>
> I: Uh, the potatoes were great. They made the meal. I loved them.

As calmly as I can, I lie. I appreciate her making my dinner, I don't want to embarrass her or hurt her feelings, and I want to remain a nice person in the eyes of everyone present, including me. So I lie. Yes, my lie is self-serving, but I rationalize that there are a lot of things worse than telling a little white lie. Besides, I'm nice, and I don't know what else to do.

AVOIDANCE AND BLUNTNESS ARE BOTH MISTAKES

In these dilemmas, either way we choose, we lose. But because we must choose, we lie to be nice. We may mouth the truism that honesty is the best policy, but when the chips are down, when we're face-to-face with people who disappoint us or don't want to hear the truth from us, we set it aside and tell little lies.

We lie so often and so consistently that we generally fail to see what it does to us and our relationships. Deep down, of course, we know that authentic relationships require the ongoing effort to increase our ability to tell truth to one another. We know, too, that when we lie to people we cannot be fully present to them and they cannot experience us in genuine ways. When we stop and think about our continuous lying, we sometimes can't stand ourselves, so we usually try not to think about it.

Back in the sixties, young people said not to trust those over thirty. One reason was that over-thirty types were nice people who did not tell you when they were disappointed, hurt, or frustrated by you. Instead, they wore fixed smiles and offered you superficial, unrewarding relationships. It was during this decade that many youth opted for blunt honesty, for "telling it like it is." They consistently gave you the truth— Wham! Bam!—right smack in your face. They "let it all hang out," and they were proud of it at the time. Now, looking back and having reflected on what bluntness did to their relationships, many of them see how selfish and ugly and counterproductive it often was.

There are people today, of course, who insist on always telling what they think is the truth. They say it is a binding moral obligation essential to their well-being. They continue to say, "With me, what you see is what you get." And they take pride in their candor. It doesn't seem to dawn on them that their perceptions may be unconsciously biased or mistaken, or that sometimes it may be more important to be considerate of others than to jam your version of truth down their throats.

We nice people may envy the ease with which these blunt truth-tellers appear to handle these dilemmas. We also, however, think that when well-meaning people come up short (when they prepare lumpy, tepid, tasteless potatoes, for example), they deserve to be excused or forgiven and handled gently. Those who run roughshod over them may think highly of themselves, but we don't think much of their self-righteousness, their rigidness, or their ability to create healthy relationships. We think they make a serious social mistake that harms both others and them.

But we also know our lying is a mistake, no matter how good our intentions are. We know that truth is essential to trust and that intimacy and functional relationships demand honesty. We show we know all this when the thought of being caught at lying, even as we try to excuse it as tact, makes us cringe. Of course, we don't lie in the first place because it's satisfying or right or wonderful. We do it because it's less painful than creating conflict or hurting people's feelings, and because we simply don't know what else to do. Sadly, it seldom occurs to us that there may be a better way.

OPTION 4: TELL THE TRUTH AND ALSO BE NICE

Since the three traditional options for dealing with hard-to-tell truth do not resolve the conflict between honesty and niceness, we need a fourth option:

Telling the whole truth with humility and sensitivity.

Before we get to the details of this option, it is important for you to decide you want to stop telling lies as a matter of course. Here again, as with the other mistakes, if you don't make this choice there's little purpose in going further. Make your commitment and write it down.

Assuming there is a satisfying way to resolve the conflict between honesty and niceness, I will no longer automatically tell little lies.

It's also helpful to tell your close friends: "I intend to remain a nice person, but I also am going to try to be honest with people from now on."

Let's assume you've made this commitment, and you've reinforced your resolution by writing it down, by posting it where you'll see it, and, perhaps, by telling others about it. We'll assume also that you understand it's more important to be strategic than spontaneous in resolving these dilemmas and are willing to exercise appropriate restraint. **You are now** prepared to take the four steps the fourth option requires.

STEP 1: ACCEPT THE PROBLEM AS YOUR OWN

Identify the *primary problem* in these dilemmas as your own failure in knowing how to resolve them. Acknowledge to yourself that the problem is yours and that you hold the key to resolving it. Until now, you no doubt have seen the problem as belonging to those who make you feel trapped. Reflect for a moment on your practice. Remember your niece's off-key recital? Was the problem her inability to sing well and be objective about it, or your inability to congratulate her? How did you see it? Can you now see it as yours?

When the hostess served me those terrible mashed potatoes and asked if I liked them, was the primary problem her bad cooking? Her need for affirmation? Her insensitivity? Or was it my inability to be honest? I didn't understand it at the time, but later I came to see that the problem was mine and it was up to me to resolve it.

In these dilemmas, we tend to occupy ourselves with how others fail us, how unreasonable they are, how their insensitivity puts us in an awkward position. We know they don't want to hear unpleasant truth; they want approval and affirmation. So it's natural to rationalize our dishonesty by blaming them: **They created the dilemma; they deserve our lies.** Yes, to blame them and tell little lies may be the best we know to do. But neither lying nor blaming does anything to resolve the dilemmas or bring integrity to our relationships.

Here is the critical first step of the fourth option: When others put you on the spot, focus first on the critical problem of your inability to know how to tell the truth. To waste time blaming them gets you nowhere. To effect a resolution that honors honesty, you must first see that the problem belongs to you.

STEP 2: ADDRESS THE ROOT OF YOUR PROBLEM—NAMELY FEAR

We say we want to be honest with those who create these dilemmas, but we're afraid to hurt their feelings. I suggest that, as with our fear of expressing our anger, there is more to it than that: At a deeper level, we're afraid that telling the truth will hurt *us* as well as them. We may be afraid of the conflict being truthful will create—most nice people live with this fear. We may be afraid people will think we are rude or ungrateful—no nice person likes to be thought of this way. Or we may be afraid they'll tell others what we said, and soon none of our friends will think we're very nice. At a deeper level, we may be terrified by the thought that they even may reject us for telling the truth. Here again, if we've claimed the promise that the universe already has accepted us, we may find that our fears have lessened or that it is now easier to deal with them, even with the terror of abandonment. But to break a longtime habit of telling little lies, we must not ignore whatever is generating our fear of telling the truth.

So each time you face such a dilemma, ask yourself, What am I afraid will happen if I speak the truth? If you can identify the fear right away, and the consequences are relatively minor, name it to the other person. If it's deep and complex, keep working at it until you track it down. Along with all other human beings, you've never wanted to look your fears straight in the face. If you're now willing to do this and bring them out in the open in this way, you'll be surprised how it will disarm or dispel them, or at least get you past them.

I'm suggesting that before you confront others with the truth of where they've fallen short or have placed unfair expectations on you, you determine the specific cause of *your* fear and name it for them:

I'm afraid to be honest with you. I am afraid to hurt your feelings and get you upset with me.
Or,
I am afraid if I tell you what I really think, you will tell our friends. Maybe I shouldn't worry about that, but I do.
Or,
I want to tell you what is bothering me, but I am afraid you will fire me (punch me in the nose, cut off our friendship, whatever).

As with the other kinds of emotionally loaded situations we've talked about, there are reasons to talk immediately about your fear. It will make your relationships significantly more honest. It also will change the way people hear and respond to you; they will not see you as arrogant, as judgmental, or as a threat. If you come down on people from a position of superiority, pointing out their failures, proffering blame, or rejecting their well-intentioned gifts, they will resent you and cut you off. But if you approach them vulnerably, confessing your fear, the chances are they will listen to your concern, rather than construct a self-protective wall around themselves.

To talk about your fear in this way is not to be manipulative and hypocritical—you don't pretend to have a problem to win their sympathy. Indeed, you *do* have a problem: You're afraid that if you tell the truth, both of you—especially you—will get hurt. Until now, you've unconsciously denied your problem and have taken the easy way out by blaming other people, by saying nothing, and by telling lies. If you now can be open about your fears, you can put these self-defeating behaviors in the past.

Here's the point: Tell others what you are afraid of and you'll be surprised at how easy it is to talk to them about what they did to set up your dilemma.

STEP 3: CONSIDER SEVERAL RELEVANT FACTORS BEFORE YOU RESPOND

Along with a history of relationship, you each bring your own personality, temperament, and life story to each particular social transaction. So before you try to tell the hard truth, answer these questions for yourself:

A. What's Been Going on between You and the Other Person?

Is this the first time this person has made it hard for you to tell the truth, or do you see a pattern? If it has happened before and you were honest, how did this person take it?

B. Who Else Is Present?

Can you be alone with them so you do not broadcast to others what you're doing? Only the rarest of circumstances permits you to tell potentially embarrassing truths to people in front of others.

C. How Does What Happened Impinge on Others?

If you're the only one who is affected by what this person has done, you may be able to take your time to talk about it. If you, however, supervise this person or you are members of a committee together, you may need to bring the issue to a head sooner rather than later.

D. What's the Person's Emotional Strength at the Moment?

Is there a healthy ego involved? What kind of a day has this person been having? You don't want to baby people, but by gauging what they can handle you show your respect and increase your effectiveness. And if the moment is not right, you can wait for a better time.

E. What's the Power Equation in Your Relationship?

Where the authority lies in the transaction will affect how you respond. Truth-telling depends on equality of respect. When you have the power, your freedom to be patient and sensitive to others' needs will liberate them to hear you. When it is they who hold the high cards— and you approach them vulnerably—you may be able to get to the truth more quickly and candidly, with less concern for their feelings.

F. How Much Truth Can Your Relationship Stand?

The amount of hard truth you can offer is in direct proportion to the depth of your relationship. This is an important point: You can be more immediately honest with some people than with others. When the woman I hardly knew served those tepid potatoes, honesty took a back seat, if not an exit. On the other hand, if Barbara served me that meal, at first taste I'd probably say, "Whoa, who killed these potatoes?" I can be immediately honest with her. Why? Not just because she has a strong sense of self-worth, but also because for more than four decades I've told her how much I appreciate both her and her cooking.

Your brain may quickly calculate these factors and free you to go on. It may also, however, leave you in a fog. For instance, you may be uncertain as to how deeply others want to be involved with you, how much honesty they'll take from you, or how soon you can resolve the dilemma. If so, you need to be aware of the tension your uncertainty creates in you, and talk about it if it's in your way. You can say, "I'm tense about where we stand with one another." Or "I'm not sure how strong our relationship is." And then you can wait for the other person to respond. You might even ask the question, "How is our relationship?" (If you offer it with a wry smile, you signal that your relationship is not only about to be tested, but also that you believe it can stand the truth it's about to face.)

STEP 4: EXPRESS RESPECT BEFORE YOU SPEAK OF THEIR FAILURE

Whether your relationship is businesslike, casual, or intimate, you are interacting with the delicate, glorious mystery we call the human spirit. If you want relationships to be rewarding, you must respect this mystery, even if others are ignoring it. Once again, if you value yourself because you know you are embraced by unconditional love, it will be easier for you to respect others and embrace them the same way. Moreover, the deeper your disappointment in them because they haven't performed well, or because they want things you cannot or do not think you ought to give them, the more important it is to express your respect for them and the value you place on your relationship.

You convey respect by your body language, the looks you give, the tone, pace, and inflection in your voice, and the words you use. If you want to tell unpleasant truths and keep your relationships healthy, you must select your words carefully. For example: You learn that a new employee, with whom you had hoped to have a growing relationship, does not have the skill or experience to take care of the matters she agreed to manage for you. You've already patiently pointed out correct ways to operate, but she doesn't seem to get it. You like her spirit, but her errors are now costing you too much time, worry, and money. A good bit is at stake here, so you might say something like the following.

> Our working relationship and friendship *mean a lot to me*. It's not easy for me to be critical of your work because I don't want to hurt your feelings

or get you upset with me. But to be fair, we need to talk about it.

Or,

I *value and respect you*, and I want a working relationship in which we can always be open with each other, as difficult as that might be at times. You have tried hard, and I appreciate that. But you've not picked up on needed changes, and we need to talk about the problems your work is creating.

If she shows immediate understanding, or says, "I want you to be honest with me," you can tell her what is bothering you. You might say:

This isn't easy for me, but I have to talk to you about our agreement. Your lack of skill and experience is showing, and I'm afraid I'm going to have to get someone else to do the job.

If your initial remarks throw her and she appears tense or upset, you may want to back off for a moment. Remember, this is a process. Sometimes it will be wisest to walk cautiously, as if on thin ice. At other times you may need to get quickly to the critical truth that set up the dilemma. In any case, no matter how slowly or quickly you get to the point, if you want satisfying relationships it will be important to demonstrate your respect for others from the very beginning.

YOUR NEW APPROACH TO TRUTH-TELLING

From now on when you feel caught in the middle between telling a lie and being honest, you will take the following steps:

1. Acknowledge the primary problem as yours: You are afraid to be honest with people about their shortcomings or unreal expectations of you.
2. Begin your conversation with talk about the specific fear that inhibits you from telling the uncomfortable truth.
3. Weigh several factors to figure out how and when and where you will begin to talk about what the other person did to put you on the spot:
   A. What has gone on in the past between this person and you.
   B. Who else is present.
   C. How what is now going on impinges on others.
   D. The person's emotional strength.
   E. The power equation in your relationship.
   F. How much truth your relationship can stand.
4. Communicate your respect for the person. Describe the healthy relationship you want and invite discussion of it. If you receive a positive response, embark on the truth-telling sensitively.

A DIALOGUE TO ILLUSTRATE THE PROCESS

Go back to our original example of the new partner at work—we'll call him Jim—whose body odor is killing you, and look at how you might handle the dilemma. You suffer with it for several days and finally ask him to stay for a few minutes after work.

YOU: Jim, before you go, do you have a minute?

JIM: Uh, sure, what's up?

YOU: I need to talk about something that's, well . . . very sensitive, and I'm not always good at this. I confess I'm afraid of hurting your feelings and of what you'll think of me. (Expressing the fear that's blocking you)

JIM: What's wrong? I'm not doing the reports wrong, am I?

YOU: No, no, you do good work, and I respect you for it. (Expressing respect for him)

JIM: Thanks. I like working with you. What's wrong?

If Jim doesn't respond this way, but reacts with wisecracks or becomes belligerent, you might respond, "I'm sorry, I've bothered you. Again, I don't do this very well," and back off. Assume, however, that he's reasonable and seems genuinely interested in hearing what's bothering you.

YOU: Well, I'm afraid I have trouble sitting near you all afternoon. You perspire a lot and by the end of the day, well, your strong body odors are difficult for me. I know it's my problem, but I don't know what to do. (Acknowledging your problem, a bit of vulnerability)

JIM: Gee, I'm sorry. I shower every morning. But, hey, it's been so hot in here, and I've always sweated like a pig.

YOU: Do you think it will help if you use a different deodorant?

JIM: I used to use a deodorant, but it didn't make any difference.

YOU: You don't use a deodorant. (A matter-of-fact statement, not a question that suggests incredulity)

JIM: I don't think they work on me.

YOU: Gosh, knowing that must be hard on you. (Empathy)

JIM: Well . . . actually, nobody's complained for a long time. Maybe I could try a new kind.

YOU: I'd like you to do that. (Saying what you want) They put new ones on the market all the time.

JIM: I'll see what I can pick up on my way home.

YOU: That's great. I feel so much better having talked. I know it must not be easy to hear something like this. I appreciate your being so understanding. Thanks. (More respect, affirmation)

JIM: I appreciate your talking to me about it.

YOU: Don't mention it. (Relieved, satisfied, happy)

Yes, this dialogue concludes successfully. And no, not all stressful encounters end as well. The fact is, any attempt to be honest can go awry and you will not resolve every dilemma. But with thought and practice, you will handle them with relative ease and the number that will end well will surprise you.

THOUGHTS ON AVOIDING DILEMMAS

Most of these dilemmas arise unpredictably, so they entrap us quickly and cause us to react in the moment the best we know how, usually by lying. But from now on, with the steps traced in the fourth option for handling truth, rather than letting such dilemmas take control of you, you will be able to respond creatively and be honest more often. In addition, there are things you can do to stop some of these dilemmas from ever occurring, or to forestall their development when they arise.

When you cultivate relationships dedicated to honesty, you will prevent some dilemmas from ever happening. As nice people, we naively and unnecessarily do not expect honesty in our relationships, we tend not to work on it, and thereby we contribute to its absence. As a result, we set ourselves up to experience these dilemmas on a regular basis. In contrast, relationships consciously committed to candor stop many dilemmas from ever arising.

As you begin to involve yourself with people, whether in friendship or as co-workers, you can initiate conversations about the truthfulness you want in your relationships. To broach the subject, over lunch or whenever there's time for a discussion, you can say something like, "I've been thinking about how niceness and honesty are often in conflict, how certain situations force us to be either nice or honest but not both at once, and how our fear of not being nice makes us dishonest with one another." You may have to explain and illustrate a bit, but most people will identify with these ideas fairly quickly and be open to exploring them further. They will no doubt have their own stories to tell about such dilemmas.

You then can say these kinds of things:

- I want you to know that I'm trying to be more honest with people without being inconsiderate and hurtful.
- I want us to be able to tell one another the truth, but that's going to take caring, commitment, and sensitivity on both our parts.
- I want you to hold up your end of our relationship, so I don't have to hurt you by being either honest or dishonest.
- If I ever let you down or want more affirmation from you than you can give, I want you to tell me.

Assertive statements like these go a long way toward establishing healthy relationships. And because such relationships are grounded in the freedom and responsibility to exchange true feelings, they lessen the possibility of these dilemmas always popping up.

Sometimes, even as you first meet people, if the situation looks like it may produce a dilemma, you can immediately set ground rules for both the situation and your relationship. Back in the early eighties, while our daughter was working in L.A., she got to know an award-winning playwright from New York who was under contract to improve someone's screenplay for Universal Studios. Because I had recently written a feature-length screenplay as part of my doctoral dissertation and was hoping to peddle it in Hollywood, she mailed me copies of his original scripts for review. A few months later when they visited us in the Bay Area, I was nervy enough to ask him if he would be willing to take the time to criticize what I'd written.

Sensing he was facing the kind of dilemma we've been talking about, he took charge of the situation. He said he would criticize it on two conditions. The first was that I would ask him to be completely honest—he said it would be a waste of his time and mine to gloss over the inevitable shortcomings of a screenplay by a novice. I knew he was right, and with a bit of fear and trembling I said, "Honesty is exactly what I want."

His second condition was that I would promise to keep in mind that he was the one who told the producers of *Saturday Night Fever* the music would never make it. And we all laughed.

As a person and a professional he didn't want to compromise his integrity by lying. But he also didn't want any honest, negative responses he might have to my screenplay either to hurt my feelings or discourage me from trying to sell it and from continuing to write. So he immediately made sure that whatever our relationship would be, it would be honest—he wanted to know whether his honesty was acceptable to me. And then he used self-deprecating humor that encouraged me not only to trust my own instincts and take responsibility for my manuscript, but also to be directly honest with him. The moment we met, he set ground rules that would help us avoid the dilemmas we've been talking about.

FINAL THOUGHTS

Even with what you've learned here, you still will not always be able to avoid these dilemmas or tell the whole truth all of the time. You cannot control all of the elements in these transactions, and on occasion, depending on the time and place and the nature of the relationship, you may conclude that being nice and lying is the best that you can do. That's where I was with the hostess who served those terrible potatoes. And when your co-worker asks you to respond on the spur of the moment to the picture of his homely little boy, it may be time to say, "He's absolutely adorable!" Realists notice this and settle for some inconsistency based on, if you will, an acceptance of their inevitable imperfection. If you can come to terms with these realities, it will save you from being cynical and unhappy with your efforts.

Of course, whenever you decide it is best to tell a lie, and you get caught, the most helpful thing you can do is to apologize immediately: "I didn't tell the truth. I was afraid of hurting your feelings and of getting hurt in return. I didn't do well by either of us. I'm sorry, and I hope you'll forgive me."

You also do well not to forget that, in spite of your inability to be honest in every situation, your very commitment confirms that you are a creative, worthwhile human being. And as you continue with the struggle to tell the whole truth whenever you can— whatever it costs and even when you fail—it will be more rewarding than automatically telling those unsatisfying little lies.

And you'll still be a *nice person*.

Mistake #7
GIVING
ADVICE

An older couple was having engine problems with a newly purchased secondhand car. They had no idea what to do. You told them to use your mechanic. They took your advice, and not only did he overcharge them for parts, he fixed several things that weren't broken. Had they not been your father and mother, they might never have spoken to you again.

When I was relatively new to my profession, a woman asked for an hour of my time and said she didn't want me to do anything but listen. I thought to myself, This is going to be a waste of time. The role models I had as a youth were professionals of all sorts who enjoyed the status and satisfaction of telling people what to do. They were professors, lawyers, doctors, and pastors who talked as if they knew all the answers. And now it was I who was professionally trained to straighten out the lives of everyone who would take my advice. Hence my thought: This is going to be a waste of time.

In spite of this reflection, I agreed to an appointment and said nothing as the woman reviewed a sad string of broken romances with men who were, to say the least, not very nice. Some of them had seriously abused her. None of them treated her with respect. Before I knew it, the hour was over; she thanked me profusely and left.

I didn't understand her gratitude. I had done little but listen. We had hardly gotten started. Then a few weeks later, I bumped into a couple of her friends. To my surprise, they reported that she was relating to a respectful new male friend, and that she had told them I had been a great help to her. That made me feel good. But what I had really wanted was the opportunity to give her some good advice.

The issue here is not the care we need to take when we offer advice. Instead it is the giving of advice itself, whether it is asked for or not, whether we mean well by it or not, and whether it is sound or bad advice.

It is in our spirit as nice people to be helpful. We give advice at the drop of a hat—whenever others ask for it, whenever we dislike what people are doing, or whenever we think they're in trouble. With good intentions, we do it to straighten them out, to get them to do what we want them to do, and to help them solve their problems:

You should go to that stop-smoking clinic.
Put your money on the Giants.
You have got to see the new Tom Hanks movie.
Take an umbrella.

Believe me. Put your kids in private school.

Hey, your car needs fixing? Use my mechanic!

We might even engage in the embarrassing self-contradiction, **"Whatever you do, never, *ever* give advice!"**

I won't *advise* you to do that. But I am going to argue that advice is never helpful and that no matter how well-intentioned or good you think your advice is, to offer it is always a mistake. I say this knowing that giving advice is as American as spending money, that almost everyone seeks it from a wide variety of sources, often paying a great deal of money for it. Advice is expected of nice people; nice people offer it all the time. I simply argue that these realities do not mean that advice serves us well.

If giving advice is a mistake, you need another way to serve those who are confused, wayward, out of control, or simply lazy. But first, to break the habit, you need to be clear on *why* giving advice is a mistake.

WHY GIVING ADVICE IS A MISTAKE

When you give bad advice you may suffer backlash. Tell your parents to get their car fixed at your repair place, and if the mechanics botch the job or rip them off, your parents end up teed off not only at them but also at you. Giving advice risks betrayal of your best intentions and can come back to haunt you. It is, therefore, not very smart. But it's a mistake for other important reasons.

Giving Advice Is a Put-Down of Others

No matter how sincere or proper or appropriate our advice may be, it demeans those to whom we give it. By telling people what to do, we imply they don't have the brains or heart or muscle to solve their problems or straighten out their lives, and we do. Rather than showing them respect and building their sense of self-worth and confidence, giving them advice tears them down and harms both them and our relationships.

Advice Fails to Give People the Real Assistance They Need

We may know exactly what others need to do to solve their problems, but they need *us* to let *them* decide what to do. This is because they need to develop their ability to take care of themselves. Again, even good advice is not helpful, for whenever you give it and encourage people to take it, and they do, you rob them of both the exercise they need to hone their decision-making skills and the satisfaction they gain by making the correct choice on their own.

In Offering Advice We Can't Be Honest

We give the single impression that we give advice to help others. But again, when we peel the layers off our motives, we often find we have more subtle, complex, and less noble interests: We may do it so our friends will admire us. We may want them to be in debt to us, be dependent on us, or even feel inferior to us. Or we simply may enjoy managing their affairs. All of us, of course, have mixed and ulterior motives—none of us is pure or perfect. But when we give advice while implying that we do it only for their good, while also serving our own unannounced, self-serving ends, we engage in a duplicity that undermines our best efforts to create relationships that have integrity.

ADVICE-GIVING IS A FORM OF CONTROL

Advice by nature bears moral imperatives: We tell others they *should* take umbrellas, they *ought to* use our mechanic, they *owe* it to their kids to parent a certain way. Even if we don't use shoulds and oughts (Use my mechanic!), we put them under the pressure of obligation: If they accept our advice, they owe us for our help. Moreover, we make them feel that if they don't do what we advise, they'll disappoint or offend us, or be doing something wrong. And if they ignore us and continue to have problems, they're afraid we may say, "I told you so" or "Don't blame me."

Trying to control others makes advice-giving a mistake. It's not our role, responsibility, or privilege to manage other people's lives. Control stifles their initiative and creativity, and erodes their self-worth. It's inappropriate, therefore, for us to take charge of them or to entangle ourselves in a struggle with them over what they do.

Sometimes we become uncomfortable with the controlling nature of giving direct advice and unconsciously try to cover it with an indirect question: "Why don't you take out more insurance?" "Why don't you put your mother in a nursing home?" "Why don't you do . . . whatever?" We think it sounds softer than the pushy "You *should* do this" or "You *ought* to do that." But the fact is that we are not the least bit interested in *why* they don't do what we think they ought to do or what we want them to do (we simply want them to do it!). So it's a false question and merely another form of coercion. Yes, it may be that we've fallen into the sloppy and innocent habit of using rhetorical questions to get others to help us in reasonable ways ("Why don't you pass me the salt?"). But when we use such questions to address others' needs ("Why don't you take out more insurance?"), we are not innocent—we are trying to control them through advice in disguise.

It's tempting to justify advice because people ask for it, including those who respect us and those whom we like to impress. But they may ask because they

- Don't want to bear responsibility for their problems—they may be lazy.
- Think they can't solve their own problems—they may be wrong.
- Are looking for someone to blame in case they take an unwise course.

So when others flatter us by asking for our advice, we cannot assume it is our obligation or in their best interest, or in ours, to give it. To the contrary, for the reasons we have looked at here, **we must assume exactly the opposite.**

TWO EXCEPTIONS TO THE RULE

I said earlier that giving advice is *never* helpful. Never? Well, hardly ever. There are two kinds of extraordinary situations when it may be fitting. The first is in the workplace, when your subordinates don't know what to do and a deadline is approaching. At such times it may be appropriate for you simply to say Do this or Do that. Even then, in order to encourage their development and deepen your working relationship with them, you will do well to relate in ways that enable them to discover their own answers or directions as much as possible, rather than have you point them out. There's an important difference between telling subordinates what to do and relating to them in ways that bring out their best. It is very clear that workers maintain better morale, relate more congenially, and are more efficient when their supervisors are not always bossing them around.

Second, there are emergencies. For example, if you see a truck bearing down on people, with no hesitation whatsoever, you can scream your advice: "Watch out! Jump! Get out of the way!" Push them to the sidewalk, if need be. But these are rare and special moments, and you cannot use them to justify giving advice in the routine social transactions you face every day.

When people you care about face problems, or are confused or lost, at a most basic level they need expressions of your love rather than your advice. They need to be sure you will never demean them or treat them as objects to manipulate—they need to feel treated as equals. When you stop giving advice you allow for meeting these needs. You also eliminate the risk, hypocrisy, disrespect, and control that are inherent in it. But then you must replace it with a respectful, effective, and satisfying way to treat them as the equals they are, and serve them in ways that are genuine.

THE ALTERNATIVE TO GIVING ADVICE

If you have accepted your acceptance, you may find it fairly easy to stop controlling those around you by offering advice. If you haven't made this decision, you'll tend to give advice almost every chance you get. Whether you have or haven't come to a place of acceptance, you can say to yourself, Now that I see that telling people what to do is a mistake, I am going to stop doing it. And as previously recommended, if you want to carry through with your resolve, write down such a statement, post it in a prominent spot, and tell your friends what you're doing.

Let's assume you do not want to continue giving advice, but you still want to serve people who are important to you when they're in need. Here are five steps you can take.

STEP 1: DETACH YOURSELF FROM THEIR PROBLEMS

The key to serving others will be your willingness and ability to back off from trying to resolve what besets them. This is not a matter of turning your back on your friends or refusing to listen to them. It is not asking you to create emotional distance from them as persons, to be partially present to them or not present at all when they need you the most. It simply asks you not to assume responsibility for their lives.

To detach is to affirm that the primary responsibility for meeting others' needs belongs to them, not to you. It means that you see yourself and them as separate and equal selves, and realize that you can be helpful only when you honor this separateness by refusing to take on their problems. Your detachment clearly tells them you respect both them and their need to make their own decisions and live with the consequences. It says you care enough about them to do nothing to prevent them from experiencing the full effect of their own behavior.

If you have a history of trying to solve other people's problems by giving advice, detachment gets you into the process of what people refer to as *letting go*. It allows you to get your bearings as someone who will no longer give advice but who still cares about others. To detach, you can immediately stop and talk to yourself, using—repeating if necessary—statements like:

> This is not my problem to solve. I'm not going to take it on.
>> Or,
> She needs to handle this, so I will not interfere.
>> Or,
> I will not rob him of the benefits of solving his own problem.
>> Or,
> If I offer advice, I will not be showing respect for them.

It may help to memorize statements like these and have them ready to repeat to yourself the moment situations arise that tempt you to resort to giving advice.

Also, you may be wise to inform family and friends about your new commitment to detach, especially the first time the kind of situation arises in which you formerly gave advice:

> Part of me would love to solve your problem for you, but I now realize that wouldn't be fair to either of us.

> I've come to see that I've been unhelpful in the past by giving you advice. Because I love you, I'm not going to do that anymore.

> I respect you too much to tell you what you ought to do.

And you often may want to add, "I'm going to be interested in hearing how you deal with this."

If you're an older person, someone perceived as wise, or one engaged in a position of authority professionally, people may come to you for advice on a regular basis and you may find the temptation to advise them almost irresistible. When this happens to me, I've found it helpful to say, "I can't tell you how tempting it is for me to tell you what to do. I'd love to make everything right and have you think I'm wonderful. But I'm not going to do that. It's going to be important for you to work this out and make your own informed decision."

Most people get the picture.

Behind detachment is your respectful assumption that the people you care about need to stand on their own feet, even when they don't want to. Thus, when you detach, you not only defeat your temptation to give advice, you also bring out the best in your friends, reinforcing their self-respect and building their self-confidence. You also, of course, make it easier on yourself by not having to worry about your advice backfiring and by eliminating any false expectations they might have that you'll solve their problems for them. And in the end, you position yourself for maintaining healthy relationships with them by treating them as real human beings.

To *let go* of the control of others may not be easy, however, because you usually must do it before you feel comfortable with it. A popular but misguided notion is that feelings are natural and actions are supposed to follow feelings, so you shouldn't do anything that doesn't feel natural or comfortable. According to this view, until you feel comfortable with letting go, you shouldn't do it. And because detachment seems to contradict what you were taught as a nice person, and because you unconsciously are so used to trying to control people, to let go will not immediately feel right or comfortable.

But there is another way to look at letting go. It calls for you to do it, whether it feels comfortable or not, and let your feelings follow. In other words, detach and *experience what it feels like to let go.* Give up control of others' lives and see what a difference it makes to the way you feel about one another. And because you can't ultimately control their lives or solve their problems anyway, it is this approach that involves no risk. The risk of hurting others and your relationships with them is not in detaching and letting go, it's in continuing to control them by giving them advice.

At this point, you may see why detaching is critical for serving others well, but you may feel stymied about putting it into practice, especially if all your life you've told others what to do. I remember how difficult it was for me the first time I relinquished control and stopped myself from offering advice. But I also remember how helpful it was—and how liberated I felt—the first time I said to myself, This is not my problem to solve. I'm not going to take it on. It also helped to realize that there were other constructive steps I could take.

STEP 2: OFFER EMPATHY

Here again, I'm talking empathy, not sympathy. When people have problems you will be tempted as a nice person to sympathize with them, to stand above them, as it were, and think, if not say something like, Oh, you poor things. But patronizing pity does not serve them well. People need you, rather, to share a sense of their predicament and their feelings. They need you to stand with them in their weakness, uncertainty, and sense of defeat. They need to know you care. So you can use your imagination to discern how you would feel in their shoes and identify it for them:

> I can't imagine anything more frustrating than
> not knowing where to turn.
> If it were my first time, I wouldn't know what to
> do either.
> I don't blame you for being confused.
> It's not easy to be a parent today.

It is important to understand that how we make people feel about themselves impacts how they feel about us and goes a long way to determine the quality of their relationships with us. Whether they are our children, spouses, co-workers, or friends, if we ignore them, we make them feel as if they don't matter, and their interest in spending time with us withers. If we try to control them, they feel smothered and resent our presence. But if we listen attentively to them (as I did with the young woman in my office), affirm their worthwhile efforts, and empathize with them when they're hurting, we make them feel valued, important, and even special. And when the way we treat them makes them feel special, they are better able to handle their lives and will want to maintain their relationships with us.

Detachment and **empathy** are always valuable. They get you off to a good start on the path to being genuinely helpful. But they often are not enough; there is more you can do.

STEP 3: ENCOURAGE OTHERS TO THINK IN TERMS OF A WIDER RANGE OF POSSIBLE SOLUTIONS

At times, people with problems bog down because they're short-sighted and haven't thought enough about their choices. If they're stalled and frustrated, you might ask casually, "You've considered other options?" If they say yes, and list them, and they omit one that might be helpful, you can follow with, "What about such-and-such? Might that work?"

If they say yes, then you've been of good service. If they say no, or they aren't sure, at least you've enabled them to expand their awareness that there might be other possibilities. If they still seem unsure of what to do,

you can encourage them to narrow their list to the possibilities that are most promising. Then you might ask,
"Which of the solutions seems best to you?" Notice that
you ask these questions from detachment; you have let
go. You don't solve their problem, make their decisions,
or control them; rather, you stand as a support alongside
them as they make their way through a dilemma.

If they identify their solution and seem ready to
make an informed, sensible choice, you've helped
them a great deal. If, however, they cannot rate one
choice as better than the others, or don't see how they
might implement the option that feels best to them,
there's another step to take.

STEP 4: PROVIDE NEEDED INFORMATION

When options do not need to be sorted out, you may
want to take this step as soon as you've detached and
offered empathy. It involves supplying names,
addresses, phone numbers, costs, times, procedures,
directions, opinions, new findings or insights, your
own testimony or someone else's, or any other relevant data. Sometimes it simply will be a matter of
telling people what you have experienced and what
you think you know.

At first hearing **giving advice** and **providing information** may sound like one and the same. In reality,
they're worlds apart: Giving advice coerces and
demeans; offering information shows respect and creates understanding.

Note the difference:

Coercive advice: You ought to buy an American car.

Liberating information: We've had good fortune with American cars.

Manipulative advice: Why don't you go to that clinic for smokers?

Helpful information: A friend says the non-smoking clinic helped him.

Controlling advice: Car problem? Use my mechanic.

Supportive information: I have a mechanic I'm pleased with.

Self-contradictory advice: Never, EVER give advice.

Congruent information: Advice is never helpful.

Giving advice creates the burden of debt. When you offer information, people not only feel no burden, they immediately feel its absence. If you can see this distinction and cement it in your mind, you make it easier for yourself to stop giving advice. And one way to do this is to put yourself in the other person's shoes, as if you're the one on the receiving end of these examples.

When you give others information, you do not demean them, you impose no obligation on them, and you do not risk a backlash of resentment as a result of misleading them. Rather, you ennoble both them and your relationships because you help liberate them to solve their own problems.

We've talked so far about four effective steps you can take: (1) detach, (2) empathize, (3) raise awareness of options, and (4) provide information. When you take them, it's possible that you'll help others solve their problems. It's also possible you won't. Their predicaments may be so complex they can't make up their minds and rise above them in healthy ways. They may be stalled by too many shades of gray and mixed feelings. If so, there's one more thing you can do.

STEP 5: NUDGE THEM GENTLY

Once they've had time to identify viable options, you can ask, "So, now, which option are you going to choose?" If they say they don't know, you can encourage them to decide by asking, "When do you think you'll choose one?"

By thoughtful, tender nudging you do not force them either to act or to select the option you prefer. You merely imply that not to choose is a choice, and that at some point they must act or take the consequences of delay. This form of prompting respects their freedom. Your purpose is not to control them, but to spur them over the hump toward solving their own problems.

It may be, if the choice is emotionally loaded, that in spite of your nudging they'll still be unable to act. They may be afraid of what you'll think if they make a bad decision. If you sense this, tell them, "No matter what you decide, I want you to know it'll be all right with me." Of course, if some of their solutions appear foolish or harmful, you serve them well to tell them: "I'm of the opinion you risk a great deal if you choose that option." Your opinion may be helpful information for them.

What you hope is that they will choose reasonable, respectful, relatively safe courses of action. To provoke their thinking, you might ask, "Which of your options don't make sense . . . don't elicit your respect . . . pose too big a risk?" In this way you encourage them to examine all possible solutions from different perspectives, and choose from the best.

THE FIVE-STEP SUPPORTIVE PROCESS IN SHORT

So these five steps offer a satisfying and effective way for you to help others:

1. Practice **detachment** in a respectful way by letting go of them.
2. Express **empathy** with their problems and feelings.
3. Ask questions that get them to expand and narrow **promising options**.
4. Provide **useful information**, including testimony.
5. Give them **gentle nudges** toward making a decision.

SUPPOSE THIS PROCESS DOES NOT WORK

If others still don't know when or whether they'll address their problems, you can do one more thing. You can empathize with their inability to decide and with their corresponding frustration:

I imagine it would be terrible not to see a way out of this.

Or,

It must be tough not knowing what to do or when you'll make a decision.

Or,

I'm sure it is hard to live with this problem and your indecision.

These last expressions of empathy may liberate them to resolve their quandaries. They may come to realize that while you are willing to stand with them, you aren't going to make their problems go away. With your support, they may decide to take a stab at their best option. If they don't, you may have to leave it at that. In spite of all you've done to treat them as adults and be supportive, they may not solve their problems. In the end, **they may not have any satisfying solutions available to them.**

Do you have any consolation in such dead-end cases? Yes. You didn't patronize, deceive, or try to control those who were involved. Neither did you generate resentment in them that would have made matters worse. These count for something. Moreover, although they didn't solve their problems, your relationships with them are more liberating and fulfilling.

TWO ILLUSTRATIONS OF THE SUPPORTIVE PROCESS

The problems people face run from the simplest to the most complex and profound. Little problems—the simple kind we stumble into every minute—beg for a quick piece of advice. For instance, when friends don't know where to have dinner in the theater district and you know restaurants like the back of your hand, it will be all you can do not to solve their problem by telling them where they *ought* to dine.

Is this harmless piece of advice worth being concerned about? It is. By itself, where friends will have dinner is relatively unimportant. But not giving advice is important to you at this point because you are trying to break the habit. Just as those who are trying to lose weight cannot look on one chocolate truffle as unimportant, you cannot think there are problems so small as to justify giving advice. When you treat anyone's problem, no matter how small, as a worthy target of advice, you weaken your resolve to change your behavioral pattern. A small dilemma is also worth taking seriously because you need all the easy practice of the supportive process you can get. When you find yourself tempted by a seemingly unimportant matter—helping friends find a place to eat, a movie to see, a plumber to call—you can use the occasion to fine-tune your skills for handling the more complex, tougher ones.

Here's supportive dialogue for when friends don't know where to eat.

FRIENDS: We want to have dinner downtown before the theater and don't want to end up in some dive.

YOU: I don't blame you. You're familiar with the good restaurants there? (**Detachment, empathy, and expanding awareness of options**)

FRIENDS: Not really. We know about Brown's, but it's too pricey. We've been to Green's once,

but there's always a wait and we want
something classier.

YOU: What about White's? (Expanding options)

FRIENDS: It's closed Sundays.

YOU: Too bad. It sounds like what you're looking
for. (Empathy) Do you know Black's Place,
on the corner of First and A Streets? It's
new, and not far from the theaters.
(Expanding options and information)

FRIENDS: What's it like?

YOU: Italian. Big pasta menu. Not cheap, but not
steep either. A bit formal, but not stuffy.
(Information)

FRIENDS: How's the food?

YOU: I enjoy it. Fresh basil in the tomato sauce.
Homemade pasta. Something like Red's
across town, but not as expensive.
(Information)

FRIENDS: Sounds good. Thanks. Maybe we'll try it.

No involvement by you in their decision. No controlling them by telling them where to eat. No attempt to
make their decision for them, and no risk of backfire.
You kept your distance, empathized with them, asked
questions that got them to expand their options, and
offered useful information. You were helpful and you
left your friendship not only intact, but strengthened.

The same supportive process applies to more complex situations, like your niece's struggle with where to
go to college. Instead of telling her where you think she
should apply, you can have this kind of a conversation:

NIECE: I can't figure out where to go to school next
year. Where do you think I should go?

YOU: I don't know, and I'm not sure I'd do you a favor by figuring that out for you. (Detachment) That's an important, difficult decision. (Empathy)

NIECE: I know, but I don't seem to be able to get with it.

YOU: Lots of people have difficulty with choosing a college. (Empathy)

NIECE: It wouldn't be so bad except my parents are almost insisting that I go to Northern, and I hate that place.

YOU: You're feeling pressed. That must make it really hard. (Empathy)

NIECE: It does. And what makes it worse is that I don't know what I want to do after that, I mean, for life.

YOU: That's not uncommon, but I'm sure it makes it harder. (Empathy) You've considered other schools? (Expanding options)

NIECE: I think I'd like to go to Eastern to get away from home, or to Central, because I have friends going there. Both are strong in engineering, which is where I have some skill, but my parents aren't impressed.

YOU: So it's between those two? (Continuing to expand options)

NIECE: I suppose. We couldn't afford Southern. And my dad's heard some really bad things about Western.

YOU: Your counselor didn't mention other possibilities? (Expanding options)

NIECE: Not really. She gave me a lot of catalogs, but I didn't read them.

YOU: You're familiar with Southeastern? (Expanding options and information)

NIECE:	I've heard of it, but I don't know anything about it. Why?
YOU:	Well, they say it has an excellent engineering school, it's not near home, and it's a state school where tuition is not out of sight. (Information)
NIECE:	I should look it up. I just haven't been able to muster the energy.
YOU:	When do you think you'll be up to that? (Nudging)
NIECE:	I don't know, but the deadline is next month.
YOU:	It must be hard to decide when you're feeling worn out. (Empathy)
NIECE:	It is.
YOU:	The catalogs may be important. Southeastern sounds like it might have something to offer. And you may be surprised at the scholarships Southern offers. (Information and expanding options)
NIECE:	I'll look them up. Thanks for the talk.
YOU:	I'll be interested in hearing what you decide. (Caring and still detached)

Again, no self-investment, no control, no pressure. You didn't tell your niece where she ought to go to school or what she should do. You identified with her struggle, raised possible options, offered useful information, and encouraged her to make a decision. You were caring and supportive.

You've noticed from both illustrations that adopting the supportive process takes longer than giving advice. To help people help themselves costs time and energy. But the reward is found in a new sense of self, in seeing the results of your efforts, and in cultivating relationships that are fulfilling.

TWO POSTSCRIPTS

1. ON GIVING ADVICE TO CHILDREN

Many nice people think it's proper for adults—particularly parents—to control children by giving them advice. Some parents see this as their God-given right and their very reason for living. But look at it with me for a moment.

Children, of course, need protection and guidance. At any time, just like adults, children may put themselves in imminent danger. For example, they may dash into traffic or play with matches. These situations call for split-second rescues, with no apologies for giving advice or controlling them. But such direct encounters with danger make up just a fraction of our transactions with children and need not—ought not—set the pattern for how we relate to them in the normal flow of daily encounters.

From the very beginning, of course, we focus on minimizing danger by setting behavioral limits for them and trying to keep them out of harm's way. We hold their hands when we near the street, and we hide matches on the highest shelf with our medicines. But limits are most effective when they are accompanied not by advice but by (1) the offer of appropriate information and interpretation ("Matches set fires. Fires can burn and hurt you.") and (2) telling them what we feel and what we want from them ("I'm afraid for your safety. I want you to tell me if you ever find any

matches."). As children increase their ability to understand us, these interpretative practices protect them
more effectively than negative advice ("Don't play
with matches!"). They also aid them in developing personally, because to offer information and tell them
what we want is respectful rather than controlling.

On an ongoing basis, when children are not in
danger but confront problems they can't handle, or
have lost their way, we can adapt the same five-step
supportive process we use with adults: (1) detach, (2)
empathize, (3) encourage them to weigh their options,
(4) provide information, and (5) nudge them gently.
The important point is that we relate to children with
respect so they develop their own skills as responsible
decision-makers.

In giving advice to children, we make the same mistake as when we offer it to adults, and for the same
reasons. Of course, with children the mistake is more
serious because they have yet to develop an independent sense of self and, therefore, are more vulnerable
to being demeaned or misled by advice. So because you
love the children in your life, just as they need to know
you will never abandon them, they also need you not
to stifle them with advice.

2. On Not Taking Advice

At times you'll find the shoe is on the other foot: You'll
be the one with problems that need attention. You also
may find yourself wanting others to solve them for
you. But you now know that to seek or take their
advice is to put yourself under their control and risk
undermining your relations with them. You see, too,

that while others often can contribute to your life they do not exist primarily to solve your problems, and, in respect for yourself and them, you need to be responsible for yourself. And you now see that taking and giving advice are two sides of the same counterfeit coin. But what can you do when you feel lost in solving a problem?

You can begin by telling friends you don't expect them to make your decisions for you or take care of your problems. You can ask them to identify with you, assist you in sorting out your options, give you useful information, and stick with you no matter what decisions you make. We all need friends who will do this.

Also, you have access to members of the helping professions—therapists, teachers, medical people, clergy, financial planners, lawyers, and all kinds of counselors. Some of them, when people go to them for help, are wise enough to be empathic, offer information, and help them learn to help themselves. You can ask those from whom you seek help to offer this type of assistance, to support your efforts instead of give you advice. In this way, you'll keep your relationships with them healthy and increase your chances of getting the help you need.

You have been so used to giving advice that you may continue to do it, even with the information and encouragement I'm offering here. When you slip, you can forgive yourself. Remind yourself you are not perfect, and look for the next opportunity to initiate the supportive process. If you practice the five steps, you will grow in your ability to avoid telling other people what to do. You also will find these new behaviors much more satisfying than giving advice.

And you'll still be a *nice person*.

Mistake #8
RESCUING
OTHERS

Fifteen years ago, your nephew, a bright and likable kid, dropped out of high school. Since then he's worked at menial jobs—or been unemployed—and been in trouble many times over alcohol. Your sister let him live at home, and regularly bailed him out of both debt and jail. But finally she says she's had it up to here. She's kicked him out and vowed not to save him anymore. So you talk your boss into hiring him.

Sometime in the late sixties, I sat one afternoon and listened to a sad young woman tell me of her fruitless efforts to save her husband, who was hooked on recreational drugs. She said the fast lane was ruining both his life and hers. As she rattled off a litany of her behaviors in their struggle, with every word she spoke I was forced to remember my own failed efforts to save a friend of mine. She said she had threatened to tell his parents, but told me she never would. I had said something similar to my friend, also without meaning it. Although she hated to do it, whenever her husband didn't show up for work because he was stoned, she called his office and said he was sick. And she never mentioned his binges even to her closest friends. I too had played along with my friend's special secret.

I'm sure that preoccupation with my own problems that hour did not serve my client well. But my reflecting on our common ineffectiveness was a breakthrough for me: It was a turning-point moment in which I came to see that in trying to serve those who are self-destructive, good intentions are far from enough.

One of the painful realities of our society today is the large number of likable people who insist on methodically destroying their lives. We all know relatives or friends who waste their education, mismanage their money, repeatedly lose good jobs, squander their time, and even destroy their health. Like everyone else, you and I, no matter how nice or intelligent we are, from time to time are self-destructive in some way, to some degree. With the people I'm talking about, however, it's a full-time, hard-core occupation. And to go on damaging themselves, they almost always manipulate those who care about them. They are experts at it. And they are the very ones we nice people try to save.

Some people adopt self-defeating behaviors out of ignorance or stupidity. Peer pressure is one reason; abuse, emotional damage, or an expression of mental illness are others. But even if several of these causes pertain to their behavior, the vast majority of people who self-destruct do it under the spell of what we call addiction.

THE CAUSES AND EFFECTS OF ADDICTION

Addictions develop when people, in order to dull some form of pain (1) engage in short-cut, substitute behaviors, or (2) abuse chemical substances (drugs). The behaviors may be ignoble, such as gambling and sexual conquests, or perfectly valid in and of themselves, such as eating, working, fishing, doing crossword puzzles, shopping, sitting at the computer, or watching TV. Valid behaviors become destructive when we use them to avoid the discomfort of facing other things we need to do, like maintain or repair our relationships, meet important deadlines, develop skills, and straighten out our lives. When we occupy ourselves with any behavior—no matter how normal—in order to avoid a struggle or pain, it inevitably threatens to become excessive and repetitive. Each of us is addicted in some way, to some degree, to some behavior, and the damage it does to us and our relationships may be relatively minor, or negligible. With many of these addictions, the trade-offs are such that even when we know they damage us, we may willingly go on with them and even live fairly functional lives.

The chemicals people use may be bought over the counter, be prescribed by a doctor, or attained illegally. People ingest, inject, or sniff these nonnutritional substances—or inhale the smoke they produce—either to numb their pain, to lift themselves up or bring themselves down, or to change their negative moods to positive ones. If they medicate in this way for extended periods of time with any frequency, they inevitably become dependent on the drugs to save them from their pain. As they do, their dependency compounds their problem: They increasingly respond to what chemical signals tell them, rather than to what makes sense or is good for them.

Repetitive avoidance behavior, including the taking of drugs, becomes a full-blown addiction as it gets more and more out of control, with people increasingly depending on it to cover pain and help them cope. Ironically these behaviors lead to far worse pain than people sought to avoid in the first place. For example, when shopaholics get the urge to splurge and go on a buying binge to chase the blues, they get things they don't need and spend money they don't have. They may get "high" in the store, but even as they do they go deeper in debt on a downhill slide that leaves them bluer than when they first went to the mall.

Addictions also damage people by requiring them to betray the truth about themselves. Someone has described addiction as behavior about which people feel they must lie to those important to them and to themselves. This self-deception, in turn, helps distort the ability of addicts to discern the difference between fact and fantasy, dream and reality. Eventually they have difficulty seeing anything, especially themselves, as it truly is. Thus, inevitably, they cannot function effectively, behave responsibly, or sustain deep, intimate relationships.

Further, addictions seduce people into surrendering the freedom they need to be responsible for themselves. Addiction is the exact opposite of freedom. Addicts think their addictive behavior will liberate them because in the early stages it took away their immediate pain. Instead, it leads them further into bondage. And at some point, even when they realize their behaviors are causing them greater pain and they need to stop, they believe they can't. They mistakenly become convinced that to abandon their addictions will cause more hurt than they can bear. And everyday, feeling more confused and less powerful, they become less able to cope with their self-destructive habits.

THE RESPONSES ADDICTION ELICITS FROM US

The destructive, addictive behaviors of those we care about disturb us:

- We lose sleep over a friend who drinks steadily and hates her job.
- A sister's eating disorder repulses and frightens us.
- We are frustrated with a colleague whose spending is driving him deeper into debt and despair.
- We worry about our teenage son who is obsessed with video games, neglects his studies, and is about to drop out of school.
- We ache for a friend who tolerates a humiliating, abusive relationship and has drifted into depression.
- We despair for our next-door neighbor who doesn't seem able to quit smoking, even as she's dying from emphysema.

Because we genuinely care about those who suffer addictions, and because we've been trained to be nice, we earnestly try to help them. In spite of our good intentions and sincerest efforts, however, their behavior usually becomes more enslaving and their lives less hopeful. This chapter contends that this happens, in part, because the approach we take as nice people is a mistake.

THE MISTAKE WE MAKE

The mistake we make with self-destructive people is trying to *rescue* them. This rescuing takes us through three predictable stages. We begin by unconsciously denying there is any problem. The thought of acknowledging addicts' shame and sharing their pain strikes us as intolerable, so we engage in wishful thinking: Surely everything will be all right. From the first moment of shock and disappointment, we turn our eyes. If we cannot escape seeing their problem, we refuse to accept it as serious. If we're forced to see it as a pressing situation, we argue in our own minds and with others that everyone does it. Or we believe there isn't any solution.

In this stage, we give addicts the benefit of the doubt about their behavior through a series of disturbing episodes. We accept whatever they tell us, even when we know deep down it's not the truth. And all along we never mention to them either their self-destructive behavior or how we are ignoring it.

It has been said that the heart is capable of infinite self-deception. We are able to pull the wool over our own eyes so that it's impossible for us to see what we don't want to face. Those of us who ignore the self-destructiveness of loved ones prove the point. Ironically, we not only deny the critical trouble they're in, but we also deceive ourselves in order to do it. Think about it: To save them from their problem, we refuse to acknowledge its existence.

In certain cases, we may have screwed up the courage to express our concern to addicts we care about but they refused to listen or got angry. So we came to feel that trying to help is a waste and, perhaps, that their behavior is none of our business. We also may be deterred by an awareness of our lack of knowledge or our own personal shortcomings. In other words, our tendency toward denial out of fear of conflict is reinforced by our fear of failure.

When we cannot sustain our denial any longer, we enter a second stage in which we control, manipulate, and even threaten addicts, using guilt and fear as our favorite weapons ("You are a disgrace!" "What would your mother think!?" "Your friends are going to find out!" "Believe me, if you don't stop, you're going to lose your job!"). It's the same control we talked about with regard to giving advice, but its expressions tend to be harsher, more extreme.

As their addictions become more threatening, of course, we step up efforts to get them in line. They resist and we try harder still. They then increase their resistance. Soon we are frustrated and angry; the whole engagement is driving us crazy. When we decide they are hopeless and we can't stand the pain another minute, as a last, desperate effort to control them we threaten to sever the relationship.

When control no longer works, we enter a third stage: We become their cover. We join them in hiding the consequences of their behavior from anyone for whom it has significance. If abuse of alcohol affects their work, we help them conceal it from the boss. If they compulsively gamble or run up bills beyond their means, we give them money on the side. If they get in trouble with the law, we quietly bail them out of jail. And in each case we help them keep it a secret. In other words, we try to save them not from the causes of their addictive behavior, or from what it does to them physically, legally, or financially, but from its social consequences. And in trying to save them in these ways, we both misdirect their energies and distract them from doing what they need to do for themselves.

The point is this: Although we may receive a great deal of affirmation from those who believe rescuing is what nice people ought to do for friends, these efforts are a mistake.

WHY RESCUING IS A MISTAKE

It Doesn't Work

No matter how hard we try, we can't change people or solve their addictions for them.

It Prolongs Their Destructive Behavior

Some authorities refer to rescuing as *enabling* because it unwittingly enables addicts to continue their behavior. In a sense, we abuse those who are abusing themselves. Here's a sad irony: With good intentions we try to get them to stop harming themselves, but instead we make matters worse. Thus, if they ever get their lives together, it won't be because of our attempts to rescue them; it will be in spite of them.

It Perpetuates Dependence on Us

Our actions rob them of the growth and pleasure they would experience if they were left—with our caring support—to solve their own problems. By taking away their power, we contribute to their loss of self-respect, self-confidence, and self-satisfaction.

It Involves Deception

Just as when we give advice, we must act as if our interest is solely in the welfare of those we're trying to help. But again we have our own interests to further: We have an interest in not being seen as uncaring; we don't want our nice family name disgraced; we want to keep everything—including people we care about—under control. Yet even when we're keenly aware of our ulterior motives, we never mention them.

It Harms Us

It allows addicts' destructive behavior to draw us into its vortex, consuming us as well as them. Instead of changing *them*, our rescuing changes *us* and our own behavior—for the worse.

IT IS ANOTHER, MORE SUBTLE FORM OF ADDICTION

Think of it this way: We rescue to avoid the pain of seeing our loved ones destroy themselves; we repeat our efforts compulsively; we want to control the situation; we crave the gratitude and gratification we think we'll receive if we save them; and we do all this without a scrap of evidence that we're being helpful and often knowing we're making matters worse. Yes, our addicted loved ones are captive to self-destructive, habitual behaviors. But here's the poignant point: *So are we who engage in rescuing them.*

It's important to be reminded that not everything that feels caring and sincere is actually helpful. A husband who abuses his wife may sincerely feel he loves her. And she may say, "I *know* he loves me." But there is a radical difference between *feeling love for her* and *loving her.* Moreover, feeling he cannot live without her is not the same as loving her. Love, which by nature liberates and never abuses, is different from the addictive and abusive need to possess and control. And we who are addicted to rescuing those who are addicted must see that, while we may sincerely care about them, to rescue is not love, but a mistake. If we do not want to continue harming addicts we love and ourselves, we must recover from our own addiction and stop rescuing them.

HOW TO STOP RESCUING OTHERS

The first step to stop our rescuing is to decide not to do it anymore. Here again, to fortify your commitment, write it down: *From now on, I will not try to save others from their self-sabotaging behavior.* Now date it and post it somewhere you'll see it every day. If you do nothing more than stop rescuing people, you'll no longer make their problems worse and drive yourself up the wall.

Of course a part of you will continue to care about them, even as they reel out of control toward self-destruction. It's important to see that to stop rescuing them is not to abandon them, and that you still have a critical role to play in their recovery. But only when you decide you will not be a rescuer anymore can you serve them well.

The task is not merely no longer to be a *rescuer*, but it's also to commit yourself to being a *nonrescuer*. As rescuer you tried to change others' behavior. As a nonrescuer, you change your own behavior in relation to them and leave any changing of themselves to their own doing. You do this because you now know they will not turn their lives around until they want to. You also know it's possible that such a moment may never come. They may never want to change.

It may help to notice that nonrescuing offers you and your addicted loved ones definite advantages. In rescuing them, you acted as if you owned them and as if they were *your* problem to solve. And your possessiveness not only showed disrespect for them, it consumed you. Nonrescuing puts a stop to that; it not only gets you out of their way, it also gets them off your back. In the same way as when you give up offering advice, you detach, step back, assume a neutral position, and **let them save themselves.** And when you mind your own business, you stop making yourself crazy, and you model a healthy, nonpossessive way of relating by which you help them learn to help themselves.

This mind-shift from changing others to changing yourself may be all you need to break the habit of rescuing. But it may not. You very well may find yourself lapsing back into denial, covering, or control—it's a way of operating that's deeply ingrained in you. Here are three steps you can take to gain the inner strength you need to avoid relapses and continue relating in healthy, nonrescuing ways.

STEP 1: WORK ON YOUR OWN CLEAR SENSE OF WHO YOU ARE

We try to rescue those important to us because our self-identity has overlapped and intertwined with theirs. In a sense, we save them to save ourselves. Thus, when we fail to rescue them, we feel like a failure along with them. In other words, the destructive addictions of people we care about control us as well as them.

You can avoid this control by seeing yourself as a separate, worthwhile being. That we are social in nature does not mean that you are not your own unique self. Indeed, that particular company of people who live in you and strongly influence you, as well as your genes and life experiences, make you the distinct person you are. No one else in the world has the same history, organic processes, personality, temperament, and consciousness as you. You are not separate from others, but you are a distinct self in relation to them, with your own makeup, identity, and value. You owe it to yourself, therefore, not to let others define or consume you. Once again, you are responsible **to** them but not **for** them—you are responsible only for yourself. So while you will **care about** those close to you who are destroying themselves, you will not live to **take care of** them.

The task is to learn where you end and others begin. You must know—and then communicate to others—who you are, what you will and will not do for them, and where you draw the lines between you. To do this, you first must accept your feelings you judge to be justified, healthy, and congruent, plus those you know or suspect are not.

If you were raised in a nice family, owning up to your feelings may not be easy; you probably learned to distrust, deny, and reject them. You may be so controlled by what you were taught as a child about what you ought or ought not to feel that even today, whenever you sense a negative feeling, you try to push it away. In fact, you may bury your strong feelings—positive as well as negative—so far down inside you that you feel nothing and are conscious only of numbness.

For instance, you may be immediately elated by a surprise in good fortune, pleased with something you accomplish, or suddenly aroused sexually by someone, yet be unable to acknowledge these pleasures. Or you may become angry with a friend, or hurt by something a family member did, or afraid of a co-worker, and be terrified by these negative feelings. But this elation, pleasure, and arousal, and the anger, hurt, and fear—plus your fear of these feelings—are all parts of who you are. And to be a genuine self you must accept them as such. Thus a primary task is to tap into your feelings, reach down inside, and bring them to consciousness. To do this, you may need to stop and become very still and listen to what your visceral regions are saying to you. It also may help then to write your feelings down and consciously claim each one as an important part of you.

Second, to be a separate self you must decide to trust your own ideas. A good way to test their trustworthiness is to submit them to people you respect. Because you were taught to find your security in the conditional acceptance of others, however, you may have kept your ideas to yourself lest people challenge, perhaps dismiss, or even ridicule them. This fear can make you hesitate to think for yourself, to express your thoughts, and to end up not even knowing what they are. And when you don't know or trust your own ideas, it's difficult to see yourself as a person who has validity. This in turn makes it hard to separate yourself from those you care about and whose approval you crave, even if they're people who are destroying both their lives and yours.

I'm not referring to your occasional uncertainty about what you think. All of us experience that. I'm talking about an ongoing distrust of your ability to generate good ideas or think clearly. To respect yourself, you must honor your mind by trusting, within reason, your own judgment.

One way to build confidence is to stop and reflect on your creative ideas and reasoned opinions and write them down. It is usually wise not to judge immediately what you think are your best or worst ideas; it's impossible for us to see the good in them from the broadest perspective or be completely objective about what we think. It's good to remember that everyone has ideas at times that prove silly or worthless. But with thoughtful reflection and the practice of writing your ideas down you can produce the clarity of thought needed to increase your self-confidence and self-respect.

And as you develop your ability to find self-validation within, rather than from others, you won't need to let your friends define who you are, to see their failures as yours, or take responsibility for their lives.

STEP 2: TELL THOSE YOU'VE BEEN RESCUING WHAT YOU ARE DOING

Whether or not you think your addicted loved ones might interpret your nonrescuing as rejection or pressure, it will help to tell them what is going on. (If you're unsure of how you'll be heard, you may want to role-play the idea with a trusted friend or counselor first.) If you now understand why you used to try to save them, you can spell it out for them and explain how you are going to relate differently:

> In the past, I've tried to rescue you from [drinking, reckless spending, workaholism, whatever]. Along with being concerned about you, I wanted you to like me. I was sincere but unaware of what effect my efforts were having. I still want you to stop your [whatever], but I won't be trying to save you anymore.
>
> Or,
>
> I used to deny, cover up, and try to control your behavior. I now see how mistaken that was and I'm not going to do it anymore. I love you and want you to stop [whatever], but you'll now have to do that for yourself.

If you're afraid they still won't understand, you can be direct about that also:

> I'm afraid you'll think I don't care about you, but I'm no longer going to try to save you from harming yourself. I did you a disservice. I'm sorry. I hope you'll forgive me. But from now on you'll have to take care of yourself. And because I love you, I hope you're able to do that.

When you go on record this way about your new way of relating, you help the others understand it, you loosen any emotional grip they have on you, and you fortify your own awareness and resolve.

STEP 3: FIND SUPPORT FOR YOUR COMMITMENT

At any time you may doubt the validity of your feelings and thoughts and be tempted to fall back into taking responsibility for those who are self-destructive. It may be, therefore, valuable to connect with a group of kindred spirits who will forgive your lapses, give you honest feedback, and encourage your commitment to nonrescuing ways.

You may find an established support group nearby. Alcohol-abuse treatment centers and Alcoholics Anonymous groups will be able to tell you where to get help. If need be, you might scour appropriate periodicals and ask around. Check the Yellow Pages. If necessary, start with a friend and create your own group. This may not be easy, and may require more courage than you think you have. But finding others to support your efforts can be an important component of changing to be a nonrescuer, and the personal affirmation you experience in a support group may fill the void and ease the pain that drove you to rescue in the first place.

BEING HELPFUL AS A NONRESCUER

You've opted not to rescue others anymore and to change yourself. To reinforce your resolve you will:

- Develop a stronger sense of self by accepting your feelings and ideas.
- Tell those you've been rescuing about your new commitment.
- Find people who will support you in your new way of relating.

As a nonrescuer—and a nonprofessional—you are now ready to help those who are self-destructive to help themselves. Look at four things you can learn to do.

1. Blow the Whistle on Their Behavior Early On

When you see others behaving self-destructively, describe it for them. Without being judgmental, point out what they're doing and how they're harming themselves. The earlier, more direct, descriptive, and specific you are, the more effective you'll be.

> You've missed several days of work due to your drinking.

You couldn't pay last month's bills and have just
purchased something you can't afford and
don't need. You are spending more than you
earn and going deeper in debt.
Your eating patterns are threatening your health.
You are using drugs and are headed for trouble
with the law.
Your smoking is affecting your voice (complexion,
health . . .)

Then tell them what you would like them to do, not
what they ought to do. Keep in mind that advice and
moralizing are not sensitive, helpful, or fair:

- I want you to get professional help for your
drinking.
- I'd like you to establish a working budget before
it's too late.
- I wish you would see a doctor about your eating.
- I want you to get off drugs and put your life
together.
- Please go to a stop-smoking clinic.

Here's the exact opposite of denial, cover-up, and
control. Instead of investing a great deal of time and
energy in saving your friends, you simply describe
what you see them doing and how it's harming them.
You neither overlook their behavior nor threaten to
leave them or accuse them of being bad. Rather, you
bring their behavior out in the open for *them*—not
you—to deal with, and you tell them what you want
them to do. Your purpose is to get them to deal with
their addiction before it takes a stronger hold.
If your whistle-blowing does not motivate them to
stop their behavior, it at least takes their addictions out

of hiding. It's no longer an unspoken tyranny or an agonizing secret. They also now know you as someone who cares enough to tell them you want them to stop harming themselves and put their lives together.

It's important to tell loved ones what you see and what you want, on a regular basis, over and over again, even if this means for the rest of your life. But it's especially timely when people you care about are in the early throes of addictive behavior.

Along with bringing their behavior out into the open, you may be able to assist them in dealing with its basic causes. Professionals in the field generally agree that beneath most addiction lies either guilt or shame or both.

2. Help Them Address Their Guilt

People experience feelings of guilt when moral codes, respected authorities, or they themselves judge their behavior to be immoral, unethical, or harmful to themselves, their environment, or others. Justifiable guilt arises when people do violate themselves or others, and it is especially powerful if they know they're doing it. (I mean justifiable, in contrast to unwarranted, guilt, which I'll address shortly.) Guilt often drives people to addiction. With sensitivity, you can help those you care about face their guilt, find freedom from their self-condemnatory feelings, and gain power over their addictions.

If addicts don't want guilt to control their lives, they need to apologize for their actions, forgive themselves, make restitution, if appropriate and possible, and stop the behavior that created it. We see the significance of guilt in its ability to alter attitudes and behavior, and thus it needs to be dealt with rather than ignored. Sadly, its positive value is lost and its power to continue driving people's addictions is magnified when well-meaning but misguided friends or counselors fail to take it seriously.

When people are guilty, you do well to acknowledge it and then forgive them. You do not help them if you either ignore their guilt or quickly condemn and reject them. Their guilt presents you with the perfect opportunity to practice the unconditional acceptance of love. In a remarkable way, by being both forgiving and candid you can help them face their guilt and then forgive themselves. If they're able to take these steps, their guilt will lose much of its grip and, with a new sense of being prized, they'll be able to develop the character they'll need to begin acting responsibly.

If guilt is driving their destructive behavior, they need to

- Acknowledge any behavior that has harmed others or themselves.
- Forgive themselves for it and make appropriate compensation.
- Stop engaging in the behavior.

To offer support, you may need to say something like this to them:

> You hurt yourself and me because of what you did with that money. I forgive you. I'd like you to acknowledge what you did, forgive yourself, and resolve not to do it again.
>   Or,
> You stole for drugs. You coped with your pain in self-destructive ways. You're not the first to do

that. And I forgive you. I want you to forgive your-self and start with a clean slate.

Persons you love may not do this, of course, and may continue their self-destructive behavior. You can never be assured that anything you do will help them save themselves. But forgiving them face-to-face, along with telling them directly what you want them to do, offers a much better chance of their transformation. Ignoring them or covering their mistakes, or trying to control, punish, or reject them won't work. So forgiveness deserves your best efforts.

And you may be required to forgive them over and over again, just like you have to forgive yourself for the foolish, damaging, unhelpful things you repeatedly do. Forgiving those who violate you time and again is not to declare their behavior acceptable. It is, rather, accepting and forgiving their imperfections so they can see your love and begin to love themselves:

> I can't stop you from continuing to steal, but I can tell you I love you, I forgive you, and I want you to forgive yourself again and get help. And I want you to know I'll support your efforts.

If you find you are more angry than disappointed, you can go back and add this to the three-component dialogue:

> When I learn you are stealing for drugs (What he does)
> I become afraid and angry (How you feel)
> because you are breaking the law and harming someone I love. (Why you feel this way)

And then you can add: "I forgive you; I want you to forgive yourself; I want . . ."

In contrast to real, justified guilt, false guilt is *inappropriate* self-condemnation. It's inappropriate because, while it may spring from any number of sources and take many forms, it's not connected to what is real. It stems from distorted pictures of the self and the world. Its seeds are generally sown by stern, overmoralizing parents and by religious authorities who use fear and guilt to control their young. The weeds it produces years later can be just as choking as real guilt. Thus it tends to destroy people who cannot rise above extreme moral teachings forced on them in childhood. For instance, some adults continue to bear terrible guilt feelings for something of minor importance they did as children ("I stole fifty cents from my mother's wallet when I was eight, and it haunts me to this day"). Still others take on guilt for their parents' divorce or even world hunger, problems they didn't cause. If people don't see this guilt for what it is, it grows in its negative power and combines with other forces to drive their self-punishing, addictive behavior.

When loved ones are bearing guilt that is obviously unwarranted, you can ask them to stop and examine it. Changing places with them might help: Invite them to judge *you* guilty for stealing fifty cents from your mother's purse when you were small, or for not saving the world, or for not being perfect. Then ask them to prescribe your punishment. If they can't charge and condemn you, it may help them see the inappropriateness of their own self-condemnation, relax, and let go of their longtime pain. If they're unable to do this, you can ask them to let you treat their guilt as if it's real and forgive them, and then forgive themselves.

False guilt is not essentially rational. So the logical thinking I have described here won't reach some people—they will cling to their self-condemnation, along with their pain and destructive behavior, and nothing you do will help them liberate themselves. For others, however, your efforts to help them get their heads on straight about false guilt—combined with your expressed concern—may help them lift their sense of worth enough that they'll be able to let go of their inappropriate guilt and start a new life.

3. HELP THEM REJECT THEIR SHAME

Shame is a much more complex emotion than guilt. And because behavioral professionals only recently have begun to take shame seriously, the debate continues with regard to exactly what it is. There is, however, a basic way to differentiate between guilt and shame that most experts agree on: When people act in a wrong way they feel guilt; when they conclude they are wrong in themselves, they suffer shame. In other words, guilt damns people for what they do; shame damns them for who they are.

In its murky complexity, some shame is healthy. It makes us feel uncomfortable for being less than we want to be, and reminds us of the gap between who we are and who we need to be. It arises naturally from within us and has positive effects. For example, when we assume we can encroach on others' rights without reproach, our shame tells us to stop and act with respect toward them. It reminds us of their intrinsic worth, of the suitable limits to our freedom, and of the tragic consequences of exceeding them. It not only checks our negative impulses and saves us from making fools of ourselves, it also goads us into channeling those impulses into constructive forms, making life safer and more satisfying for everyone. If those who traded in slaves, perpetrated genocide, and tortured and raped their way throughout history had felt this kind of shame, humankind would have been spared much suffering.

But the shame we're concerned with here is not the healthy restraining force against destructive behavior. In contrast, this shame restrains people from doing what is healthy, constructive, and needful. At the least, it distorts how they see themselves, as if they're peering through glasses whose lenses are dirty, out of focus, or broken. This shame exaggerates their shortcomings and won't let them see anything good in themselves. So in their eyes, they never measure up to their own idealized selves or to the people they admire.

At its worst, this shame annihilates people's self-worth, poisoning them with self-hatred and infecting them with what someone has called *a sickness of the soul*. They commit a single act of which they're ashamed, and they feel wretched, believing they are terrible persons. They judge themselves not simply *undeserving of special favor* (which all of us are), but *worthless* (which none of us is). In a negative cycle of self-criticism and unable to tolerate themselves, they tend to sink into self-loathing and addictive behavior, wallowing in the anguish of their shame and using whatever they can find to dull its terrible pain.

People smitten by shame inevitably distrust themselves and others, including those closest to them. Thus they do not form healthy relationships and tend to live desperately lonely lives. Lacking the support of respectful community, their antisocial self-destructiveness tends to go unchecked. Accordingly, they suffer a pro-

found sense of disconnection while striving desperately, and usually unsuccessfully, for the slightest sign
of approval from, ironically, the very people they seem
unable to trust.

To be liberated from their addictions, your shame-
stricken friends must understand that it is not they
who are worthless, but their shame. It's your privilege
to help them discover this truth and make choices that
help heal their wounds. It's critical to remember that
your task is not to save them, but to be fully present to
them as persons, to listen sensitively to their pain, and
to be patiently empathic. To this end, while you do not
condone their self-destructive behavior, you can listen
without judgment, tell them how much you love
them, and promise never to reject them, offering
repeated warm embraces and verbal affirmations as
necessary. They may need constant reassurance.
Because they are bound by shame, they also may
never be able to trust you. But you go a long way
toward building trust if you show them you accept
them for who they are and will stick by them no
matter what. And it will help convince them you are
caring, nonjudgmental, and worthy of their trust if you
are clearly respectful whenever you refer to others
who are self-destructive. In the end, evidence that they
are loved in spite of the mess they are making of their
lives and the pain they're causing you is the most
beautiful gift you can give them.

Once you have won a hearing, at an opportune
moment you can encourage them to identify the
source of their shame and bring it out in the open by
naming it to you. This may not be easy for them.
People usually find it harder to deal with shame than
with guilt. It inflicts deeper wounds and leaves larger
emotional scars than guilt feelings, and rather than

arising naturally from within the self, it is evoked by a variety of outside forces that most shame-driven people do not see and try not to think about. For them to reflect on what causes their pain may require them to face difficult truths about themselves. So they tend to remain ignorant and secretive about their shame, allowing it, ironically and tragically, to increase its power. When they are willing, however, to look for the specific source of their shame, to see it and name it to you, the reverse happens: Their shame loses much of its strength and becomes easier for them to face and reject.

Three forces stand out as creators of destructive shame. Look at them and at how you can help people begin to defeat them.

1. The Social Prejudices—Racism, Classism, Sexism, and Heterosexism

These negative judgments wrongly make people feel ashamed of their skin color, economic level, gender, or sexual orientation. They stigmatize them for factors over which they have virtually no control and for which, to begin with, no one has a right to make them feel shame. We need not look far to find addiction and self-destructive behavioral patterns among those who take their identity from social groups that have been ostracized or denied their full humanity in some way.

If your friends suffer from this shame, you can ask them not to believe they are worthy of self-condemnation based on race, social class, national origin, sex, or sexual orientation. If they cannot do this and are unable to affirm themselves, you can do it for them; you can tell them how much you value them for who they are. You also can ask them whether they think other people should be ashamed of who they are, and, if so, why? Along with your loving affirmation, such a direct, gentle question may help them begin to see that their shame is unnecessary and worthy of dismissal.

2. Maltreatment by Parents When They Were Children

If those you care about felt threatened by rejection or were abused in any way by parents or siblings, as adults they still may feel unworthy of respect or of a good life. If the abuse was kept a family secret, the shame no doubt deepened, and to this day they may be mortified to be who they are. You can identify with their pain, saying, "It must be terrible to have those memories and feelings." You then can ask them to accept their wounds, to let them heal rather than pick at the scabs, and to envision the scars and the pain fading away. Damaged as they may be, if they are to liberate themselves from their addictive behavior, they must refuse to live as victims of the past and make a new start in life.

3. Social Standards that Define Them as Failures

Our society suggests that if we lack wealth, power, vocational status, or fame, we have not succeeded. Many people too readily accept this judgment, defining themselves by their failures and dwelling on them. Unfortunately, family or friends often reinforce their perspective, constantly telling them they're bad or weak, comparing them to others and putting them down all the time. And whether they measure up or not, the shame of never being good enough haunts them night and day.

If your friends suffer from this shame, you can help

them break their negative self-definition by refusing to see them as failures and telling them so. You can remind them that shortcomings are normal and unavoidable, that there is no shame in being human—which is to fail at times—and that they do not need to demean or reject themselves. If they don't take your prodding, you might ask them to see their failures as teachers, giving themselves the opportunity to learn from them, instead of being defeated by them.

You also can talk to them candidly about your own failures, making it clear that you are someone who (1) is worth a great deal simply as you are, (2) has done things for which you are ashamed, and (3) has chosen not to let your defeats and shame control your life. Engaging in humor about your failures may help them decide not to take their own too seriously. You can tell them that no one is more successful at failing than you are. For them simply to see you comfortable with your shortcomings may help liberate them to accept themselves.

If they show an immediate desire to get rid of their shame but after a while don't seem to be making progress, you can ask them to get professional help, perhaps giving them the name or number of a counselor or local treatment center that specializes in addiction and shame.

3. INTERVENE WHEN THEIR ADDICTIONS THREATEN TO DESTROY THEM

Shame-bound addicts may be unresponsive to your best efforts along the lines we've been talking about. They also may accelerate their use of drugs to the point that it creates serious financial, legal, or health problems and leads them, usually blindly, into a final downward spiral. If they follow this course, it's important to understand that before they can avoid complete self-destruction, they must stop abusing themselves with chemical substances. If their finances are in chaos and they're using alcohol to cover their pain, they must quit drinking before they can straighten out their money. Stopping their drinking won't solve their money problems, but if they want to resolve them, they cannot continue to drink. It's critical to see the significance of their substance abuse and focus first on getting them the help they need to stop.

Sadly, those addicted to drugs tend to use them until their jobs, marriages, children, or very lives are at risk. If you early on call them on their behavior and support their efforts to deal with their guilt and shame, you may help free them to stop before they lose everything, including, perhaps, their lives. Or you may not.

When substance abusers reach a crisis stage, one of three things happens: (1) The drugs kill them or they take their own lives; (2) they decide on their own to begin the process of recovery, or (3) their loved ones force them to get help.

Indeed, the crisis stage may call you to initiate what is called **an intervention.** *Intervention* is the official term for the process used to get addicted loved ones to commit themselves to intensive professional care before they harm themselves irreparably. You start the process as soon as you see signs of imminent danger— an alcoholic friend blacks out from drinking or a drug user in your family turns to stealing. Such signs call for a justified, emergency rescue operation. It's the last step before you talk to a lawyer or call the police. And it may be up to you to start the process.

Fortunately, you do not have to tackle this task

alone. An intervention may be initiated by the boldness of one person, but we've learned that it's best accomplished with the support of family members, close friends, and others who care. It also involves the supervision of an experienced professional.

Before loved ones confront an addicted family member or friend through intervention, they meet to agree upon the specific signs that point to imminent danger. Signs include violations of the law, the inability to sustain a job, needless money crises, menacing physical or mental ailments, and serious damage to relationships. At the intervention itself, those present begin by reciting the identified signs, doing so to justify their insistence that their addicted loved one gets serious, professional care. They also serve notice that until there is commitment to recovery, their normal business with that loved one will cease. At the same time, they pledge themselves to stand with this person through the recovery period and be there when it's over. Interventions are hard. They also are not always successful. But they sometimes make the difference between life and death.

It often takes just one caring person to recognize a loved one's crisis, to break the conspiracy of silence about the addiction, and then to get on the phone and organize an intervention. The point is, when someone you care about is in danger, you are not alone; there are experienced professionals available. A local treatment center can put you in touch with assistance.

YOU HAVE NEW WAYS TO HELP

You now have constructive ways to relate to those who are addicted and self-destructive. You will

- Describe their behavior early on and tell them what you want them to do.
- Forgive them their guilt and ask them to pardon themselves.
- Encourage them to identify, expose, and reject any shame they're bearing.
- Initiate an emergency intervention with professional help.

These nonrescuing efforts, of course, may not work. As you've always known, no matter what you do, you still have to live with the pain of those whose addictions overpower them. You also may be criticized by friends you refuse to save and by others who still believe in rescuing. And very likely you will have to bear uncertain feelings about whether you are serving those you care about well. But at least you will no longer be making things worse for them and for yourself by *enabling* them to continue their destructive behavior.

It may be that some of your addicted loved ones will accept your love and turn their lives around. Your refusal to rescue them, along with your accepting spirit and respectful directness, may free them to save themselves. And thereby, you not only will keep your own life on an even keel, but you also will be in a good position to support and enjoy their recovery.

And you'll still be a *nice person*.

Mistake #9
PROTECTING THOSE IN GRIEF

A good friend's husband drops dead of a heart attack. You rush to her home and find others trying to offer comfort. All she can do is sob and talk about her husband's smoking and his failure to exercise. You explain that to cry and get angry doesn't do any good, and she ignores you. You try to cheer her, but without success. You tell her she has to be strong for the kids, but she goes to pieces. And you end up feeling you should have stayed at home.

I suffered my first intimate experience with the anguish of grief with I was ten. My grandmother, Anna, my father's mother, lived with us in a large, suburban Philadelphia household along with my parents, my three older sisters, my mother's half brother, and me. Her husband had died thirty-one years before, and she, at seventy-five, was still working hard hours as a matron in the women's prison in the city. Everyone respected and loved her. Early one morning, Anna went to work as usual on public transportation but, not feeling well, soon came home, lay down, and later that morning died. I was home and heard about it immediately, but my parents saw to it that I was kept out of the house all day. Because I knew what had happened, I felt sad and cut off during those hours. I remember how helpful it was that evening to cry with the rest of the family.

The second poignant day of grief for me came seven years later. In March of 1950, right before I was to graduate from high school, my mother, who was fifty-four, broke her hip in a fall from the tall, top step of a trolley car. Ten days later, on the day before she was to come home from the hospital and one day after she said for the first time that she was beginning to feel like her old self, a blood clot lodged in her heart. She died quickly and quietly. The news hit us as an awful shock. It was probably the worst day of my life.

I first learned what had happened when the principal called me to his office from fourth-period class. There, my father, his pastor, and my sister Isabel were waiting. The moment I looked at their faces, I knew what they would tell me. I can only remember crying, "Oh, *no!*," and I think I said, "It can't be, no, no, *no!*" Their long, strong yet trembling embraces and the mixing of their tears with mine carried me through those first moments of excruciating pain. When we arrived at the house, my other sisters, Ella and May, and I hugged and cried. My parents' friends soon began arriving, some with flowers or food, some simply with their willingness to share our pain. Their presence meant a great deal, especially to my dad. After a long afternoon of sitting around with a lot of older folk, my sisters persuaded my dad to let me take the car and spend some time with my girlfriend. That evening, we sat in the car in front of her house while I sobbed and she simply held me. Down through the years I often have wondered how I would have gotten through those first awful hours of grief without such support.

FACING INEVITABLE GRIEF

Grief is the painful adjustment we all must make when something goes wrong or threatens us. We must adjust when a loved one dies, when we receive bad news about our health, lose a valued job, or go through a personal rejection. Since things, both large and small, go wrong in our lives every day, pain pervades the human condition and life, in a very real sense, is grief.

This chapter focuses primarily on the devastating grief people bear upon the death of someone they care about and how you relate to them. It will prepare you to respond effectively when

- A good friend's husband drops dead of a heart attack.
- A co-worker's mother dies after a long, debilitating illness.
- A neighbor is killed when her van is blown into traffic in a storm.
- A longtime friend is depressed after a miscarriage.
- Someone calls to tell you his little girl has suffocated in her sleep.
- Your child's favorite teacher dies of AIDS.

Fortunately we do not face such intense encounters every day. We are constantly haunted, however, by the awareness that sooner or later one will overwhelm us. And when those times come, we want to be able to say the right words, to effect a manner that consoles, to approach the bereaved with what might be called a *sacred sensitivity*. Yet, we live in a society that works hard to avoid the realities of death and dying, we're never given classes in school about grief, and have little experience with it at such emotionally charged levels. So even before we are tested by such encounters, we feel inept and ill at ease.

To make matters worse, we know that when these moments arrive and we draw close to the bereaved, we can expect their speech and demeanor to bewilder us. Their moods may change dramatically. They may appear calm when they feel shattered and upset, or laugh out loud when their pain is unbearable. If they're in shock, they may not even know what they want from us. Worst of all, as they desperately try to cope with their grief they may expect things of us we cannot deliver.

The thought of being touched by their enormous pain can be so disturbing that we may be tempted to stay away and simply wring our hands. Usually, of course, both our niceness and compassion compel us to go to them and, for better or worse, to do our best. And unconsciously we assume that because people have survived these situations since the beginning of time, if we do our best to copy what everyone else does, we'll get by. Yet here's the rub: No matter how good our intentions are or how hard we try, we most often end up feeling that our efforts are not helpful. Sometimes we even add to the pain of those who grieve.

You possess the ability to connect with the bereaved at the deepest of levels; it's within all of us to do this. And you can learn to be genuinely helpful in the face of grief so that you feel satisfied with your efforts. To get started, you need a basic understanding of grief as a process.

GRIEF AS A PROCESS

Most people think of grief solely as the profound sadness that results from a serious loss and that leads to mourning, that is, to conventional, acceptable expressions of sorrow. But professionals who specialize in grief and mourning tell us it is more complex than that. First, they contend that there is no single, universal prescription for mourning—no simple, one, right way to do it—and that we all mourn differently, usually following family traditions and adapting the practices of our particular sub-cultures.

Second, they define grief as the dynamic process of painful adjustments we must make when faced with an unhappy reality. The process of grieving, they say, almost always takes us through a series of identifiable emotional and mental stages, or defensive responses:

1. **Denial:** "Oh, no, it can't be!" Or "There must be some mistake!"
2. **Anger:** "This is unfair! Why in the hell did it have to . . . ?"
3. **Bargaining:** "O God, if you get her through this, I will . . ."
4. **Depression:** "Life is not worth living. I can't go on."
5. **Acceptance:** "I suppose I can—and I might as well—go on."

Third, professionals differ on the nature, names, and order of these stages. They observe that the bereaved do not always experience the first four of them in order, or even in linear sequence, and that sometimes they seem to go through them all at once. They also may become stuck for a period in one stage or another or go in and out of the five stages many times. Sooner or later, however, before they reach the fifth stage of accepting the painful reality and getting on with their lives, if they ever do, it's generally agreed they'll go through—and it's important for them to go through—the first four stages in some way, to some degree, whether they're aware of doing it or not.

Once we understand grief as a natural and normal process—and a valuable source of growth—we can be patient with others as they try to recover from their losses. We can be sensitive to the power and complexity of what has impacted on them and relate to them appropriately, even at the deepest levels, as they make their way through the various stages. It is in seeing grief as a process that we have the foundation for relating helpfully to the bereaved and for feeling more satisfied with our efforts to be helpful.

Now stop and look at the common mistake nice people unconsciously make as they relate to those who are grieving: **the practice of** *protection.*

THE TACTICS OF PROTECTION

When people who are important to us suffer the death of a loved one, we want to shield them from their profound pain. The avoidance of pain concerns us; and we like to think of ourselves as considerate if not compassionate. We assume that to protect people in pain is the loving thing to do. The practice is reinforced because most people in grief prefer to be protected rather than have their pain continue. Moreover, popular opinion supports the tactics of protection we predictably employ.

I call this protecting a mistake because, just like giving advice and rescuing others, it fails to offer the bereaved what they need and slows their recovery. At the same time, because it enjoys as much social approval as these other two mistakes and is always offered sincerely, we don't see it as a problem. It also escapes critical analysis because it often is mixed in and confused with healthy and helpful responses to the bereaved. So before we go further, it's important for us to clarify exactly why protection is a mistake. To do so, look at the tactics we commonly use with the bereaved, what these tactics do to them, and why, in the end, they fail to work.

To begin, almost all of us try to appear strong when face-to-face with grieving friends. We act as if we know what we're doing, even though we don't. We're terrified that we're about to say the wrong thing, but we pretend to be calm. We project confidence even though we are apprehensive about our ability to do the right thing and save others from their pain.

Of course our manufactured appearances are false, and by our pretense we build an invisible, impenetrable wall between the bereaved and us, rendering ourselves both unreal and unknown to them. Moreover, when they falsely perceive us as strong, they are made more aware of their own weakness. Thus we make them feel isolated, inferior, and, as a result, in some cases, resentful. And in the end, we go away feeling not only inadequate, unsatisfied, and cut off from the widest range of our own emotions, but also estranged from the very people we try to protect.

At a conscious level, our attempts to appear strong are supposed to encourage those in grief to be strong, too. The idea is that if we exude strength, we will help them keep their composure. The last thing we want them to do is go to pieces. We don't want them to embarrass themselves or be unable to cope with the many ordeals they will have to face. But we also come on as strong because the immediacy of another's death threatens our emotional security and makes us feel vulnerable inside to the terrible pain of the bereaved. Any emotional breakdown on their part would remind us of, and make us anxious about, the tragic side of life and the fact that we ourselves must one day die. So without thinking, we play being strong to protect ourselves.

Of course, to acknowledge this anxiety at the time—even if we were aware of it—is difficult. It is important for us to see, however, that when we create emotional distance from others to cover our own anxiety, we not only dupe ourselves into thinking we can help them while remaining aloof from their pain, but we also treat lightly the profound feelings of the very ones we say we care about. We betray our own authenticity, our best intentions to be helpful, and the bereaved themselves.

A second protection tactic is silence. Nice people often engage in an unspoken pact never to mention the death to the bereaved. (It's the very same silence we adopt when face-to-face with those who have been told they are terminally ill, or have been given some other terrible news.) We assume that not to mention it avoids deepening their pain or helps them to escape it. But instead, while perhaps temporarily enabling them to sidestep the terrifying, central fact that a loved one has died—a reality with which they need to be coming to terms—

our silence delays the process and prolongs the pain.

A third tactic is small talk. We use it to distract them. They have suffered a precious and irretrievable loss and feel deep pain. Uncomfortable with that pain, we may chatter when we don't know what to say or have nothing worthwhile to talk about. We may comment on the traffic, the weather that delayed us, something we recently saw on television, or other matters of no immediate significance.

One day the staggering shock will subside and the bereaved will attempt to go on with their lives. At that time, they probably will need to talk about more than their loss, and for us to bring up other subjects may be just what is needed. But when they are suffering the first pangs of the painful news, talk usurps the time they need to grieve and intrudes on their mourning.

A fourth protective tactic is the use of euphemisms. We hope they will stave off or soften the intrusive vulgarity of the death. Rather than identifying the deceased by their names, we tend to refer to them by their roles (your wife), or use pronouns (him). Or you often hear something like, "I'm sad to hear she *passed away.*" Or "I was so sorry to hear you *lost* your husband." Protectors find it impossible to say, "I am really sorry to hear that Fred died."

Euphemisms can do harm in three ways. One, grieving friends may resent us and our indirect, impersonal language for what it is, thought they probably won't mention it. (Have you ever heard a widow say, "I didn't *lose* my husband, for heaven's sake, he *died!*") Two, euphemisms may cause them to distrust any help we offer because they'll think we've not caught the gravity of their situation. Three, wanting themselves at one level to deny what's happened, they may use our euphemisms to help postpone facing the painful

240

feelings they desperately need to be working through. A fifth approach is to cheer them up. We may say things like, "At least he didn't have to suffer too much." Or "It could have been a lot worse." Or even "You are fortunate to still have your other two kids." We want them to look on the bright side, even if we have to invent one. We assure them that everything will be all right, even when we don't know what we're talking about. Here again, not meaning to do so, we tell them their pain isn't valid and they're wrong for hurting as they do. When we cheer the bereaved, we discount the very feelings that overwhelm them and thus make it harder for them to grieve.

Sixth, protectors give the bereaved advice: "Don't let the kids see you cry," or "As soon as this is over, get away for a good vacation." As advice always does, it diverts their attention from finding their own solutions. It patronizes them, as well as being dishonest, and is an attempt to control them. Advice is a particularly serious problem here, because in trying to control the bereaved we risk leading them astray in their grieving. Even if our advice steers them in sensible directions, it runs counter to their responsibility for their own recovery and can burden them, in addition to their grief, with feelings of inadequacy, stress, and false guilt.

A seventh tactic of protection, particularly by those who are religious, is the appeal to platitudes: "It's God's will," or, "We will miss her but we know she's in a better place," or the common, "I'm praying for you." (Even nice, nonreligious people tell the bereaved they're praying for them, whether it's true or not. It's an indirect attempt to tell them we care and will not forget them.) The bereaved have something to be in pain about, of course, and this is another tactic that distracts them from experiencing the full impact of their loss and attending to their sorrow. (This tactic at its worst is the insensitive effort by religious zealots to convert the bereaved to religious faith, manipulating them in their most vulnerable moments for what we might call the ultimate protection.)

An eighth tactic we often use is the innocent offer, "If you need anything at all, don't hesitate to call." We want those who are suffering grief to think everything will be all right because we will do anything for them, even though there are things we won't do. We would like them to think there is no problem too big for us to handle, although we know it's not true. But when we offer to do *anything at all,* they may call on us for things we can't do, or won't do. If they do ask, we may resent them. In not doing what they ask, we betray our declared interest in serving them and add frustration to their grief.

Finally, protectors often press the bereaved to rush their grief. We imply that if they're strong, they will move through it quickly. After a while we may ask, "How long are you going to mope?" or tell them, "You have to stop feeling sorry for yourself and get on with your life." We may expect friends in three months to shed their feelings for relationships built up over years, and thus make them feel guilty for grieving. But under our pressure to put their loss behind them, they may bury their grief and both miss its lessons and damage their health.

In the end, no matter how sincere we are, the tactics we use to protect the bereaved do not work. They fail because they cast us in the false role of protector, they tend to sabotage the grief process, and they divert us from offering genuine consolation. If you see the damage protection does and what a mistake it is, the next time you are privileged to be with the bereaved, **you can decide not to:**

- Pose as strong and invincible.
- Avoid mentioning the death.
- Chatter about things that don't matter.
- Use euphemisms.
- Try to cheer them up.
- Give them advice.
- Engage in sentimental platitudes.
- Offer help you can't or won't deliver.
- Rush them through their grieving.

But if you will no longer protect those who suffer grief, how will you relate to them?

AN ALTERNATIVE TO PROTECTION

Contrary to popular myth, the simple passing of time does not relieve crippling sorrow or heal deep wounds. Time helps, but only grieving and mourning do the healing.

Death shatters the emotional security systems of the bereaved and they often go into shock. At the same time, their lives are dramatically slowed down, even stopped, giving them time to absorb the significance of what has happened. These hours in themselves can be frightening and painful, but they must not be ignored and wasted. To pick up the pieces of their lives and eventually move on with a restored joy, they must use this time to grieve, to endure the painful, often difficult adjustments we looked at earlier. They also must mourn in ways that release them from the power of their pain, heal their wounds, and get them beyond their debilitating sadness. To mourn, someone has said, is to mend. And mending is what everyone needs when someone dear to them dies and they must go on without that person.

Our task is to support them through this painful grief process.

SUPPORT FIRST MEANS YOUR FULL PRESENCE

If you want depth in relationships with the people you care about, you must learn to be fully present to them on an ongoing basis. As we saw earlier, it is not mainly a matter of tactics, techniques, and accomplishment, but the essence of relating authentically, the most human way to be with others. I suggest now that it's exactly what is called for in times of crisis and painful grief. And fortunately, even if your relationship with those who are grieving has been distant, stilted, or shallow, you can make a commitment to be fully present to them in these special moments.

First of all, full presence is what people mean when they talk about *being there* for others who need emotional support. This is not always easy, of course, because exactly when people will need support is unpredictable and much of the time we must **be there** for other people who are important to us or for ourselves. So we cannot promise everyone we care about that we'll **always** be there for *them*. We can be sensitive to when and where we're needed the most and make the most thoughtful choices. And if we're honest with friends about when and for what they can and cannot count on us, then whenever we're with them our presence will be total, our interactions will be genuine, and both they and we will be richer for it.

Full presence means attending to the needs of the bereaved rather than your own. You cannot offer the support they need if you're preoccupied with impressing them or making sure others know what a wonderful person you are. As you enter their presence, you must set aside your own needs and agendas, and go with what is given by the situation. Before you step in the door, it will help to find out what's going on inside you, to identify consciously why you are where you are, and then to focus on being the person you need to be.

To be fully present you must approach the bereaved as a human being—one who, like them, suffers pain—and not as a superhuman savior. The task is to be with them as a caring, vulnerable friend rather than as one who pretends to know all the answers and who is afraid to reveal you're afraid. It may strike you as odd, but being fully present requires you to accept the paradox that you are genuinely strong only when you can show your weakness.

This paradox, of course, shatters the popular myth that to be strong you must not be weak and that, if you feel weak, you must hide this feeling when you're called upon to be supportive. And strange as it may seem, by revealing your weakness, you pass along your strength to those who need it. When they feel broken, they gain support and healing from us if we can acknowledge that we, too, are in pieces. When they hurt, they draw comfort from the closeness of others who can identify with their sorrow and pain. And because you cannot do anything to undo the death, you must accept not only the reality of the death but also your inability to take away their pain and the insolubility of their problem.

To be present in any genuine way also involves suffering silently with them. Even after your silence has given them time to articulate their feelings, the less you talk the better. For one thing, people in shock hear very little anyway. No, you do not ignore them or fail to acknowledge their loss. But you avoid filling the quiet moments with chatter. And your endurance of difficult times of silence speaks volumes about your care. It says to them, "I will not control you. I have no easy answers but I'm with you. I am not giving up on life or on you."

Full presence also requires you to connect with them in ways that encourage them to experience and express their pain. Listen patiently and quietly with your heart. Your attention will let them feel they do not have to hide their negative feelings. If they sense you are listening to them—especially to what they are *not* saying—they will feel your oneness with them and perhaps be more open about what they are experiencing.

Eye contact will tell them you are there, close to them, not to take away their sadness but to share it. In their eyes you will see most clearly what they are feeling, especially when they're unable to speak. And if with words they tell you they're doing fine, moisture in their eyes will tell you of their pain. If they allow you, you can let your eyes meet theirs, looking through them to embrace, and then reflect back with your eyes the sorrow you don't want them to bear alone.

Note also that there are **things you** *cannot* **do** if you want to be fully present to those in grief. For one, you cannot feign weakness or put on the appearance of pain to comfort them or impress them with your caring. If you genuinely share their grief, your honest

246

tears can liberate them to be true to their sorrow and override any expectations they have that they must appear strong and not cry. But your confessions to be at a loss and any crying you do must be authentic. You cannot pretend anything and be fully present.

You also cannot let their grief overwhelm or consume you. You need to be fully but not overbearingly present. You do not want them to have to take care of you but to be free to mourn in ways that are liberating to them. So it's important to act in ways that show you are responsive to the fact that they are in great pain, while at the same time not allowing yourself to be emotionally overcome by their grief. Too many mourners have been additionally burdened by well-meaning friends who cannot relate appropriately to their own grief.

Then, too, you cannot be fully present and spend any time judging what the bereaved say and do. When our efforts to help don't work, our task is not to stand back and focus on their lack of progress: "Boy, she's still in the **anger** stage." "Gosh, he's certainly dragging out his **depression**." "I can't tell whether they've moved on to **acceptance** yet or still are stuck in **denial**." We must take them as they are and grace them with our compassion and understanding. They need friends to be direct yet gentle with them. The last thing they need is judgment, advice, or criticism.

In situations of grief, you may be more able to be fully present if you've accepted yourself by accepting your acceptance. In these intensely painful moments, it's always tempting to lapse back into trying to appear strong or impress your grieving friends with how helpful you are. If you feel secure in the love you've found at the heart of the universe, you can be more at ease, and natural, and further able to avoid unhelpful behaviors.

BEYOND FULL PRESENCE AS SUPPORT

Suitable physical touch can nurture closeness and healing, and express the warmth of your caring. Sometimes it is fitting to offer the long, close embrace, the kind that allows people to let down and sob while you hold them. As you quietly listen to their story, it may suit your relationship to sit and hold their hands. You do not want to force your touch. Your purpose is not to create in that moment an intimacy that does not exist, or to coerce them to mourn. Indeed, inappropriate touch can leave them confused and uncomfortable. The task is to be sensitive to what they are receptive to and signal what you'll offer through the softest gestures and subtlest body language. If you are uneasy about how they may interpret any physical contact on your part, suspend the idea and don't worry about it.

While eye contact, attentive listening, and appropriate touch are your initial allies, the time may come for a few words of support. But what words? You might tell them what you're feeling. If you feel awkward and it's getting in the way of being fully present, you can say, "I feel so bad about what you're going through, but I feel awkward and don't know what to say." If you feel tense for fear of saying the wrong thing, you can say, "I'm afraid of saying the wrong thing, but if you'd like me to stay with you, I'd like to do that."

The fact is, there is much here that is beyond your control, and it's generally helpful to acknowledge this. It also may be helpful to share your own experience of grief, if you can. Over the years, those who have been most supportive to me with their words are not those who tell me what to do or impress me with what they know, but those who, after holding me and listening to me, can be personal about their own vulnerability to both their grief and mine. Perhaps you can say, "I feel terrible about what you're going through." Or "It makes me so sad to think of your loss."

To move beyond simply revealing your limitations, you might imagine what else you would want to hear in the way of support were you in their place. Think about the times you've been in pain, and identify what others did that was helpful. It will help, too, if you can be sensitive to the emotional clues they give off. Again, empathic words that reflect acceptance of what they are feeling are always healing. Here are some suggestions about what to say:

When you sense an overwhelming *sorrow*: "This must hurt terribly."
Once you hear *anger* in their voice: "I don't blame you. I'd be angry, too."
If you discern *guilt*: "You did what you could. None of us is perfect."
If you sense a *fear* of the future: "It must be scary to go through this."
When they seem *confused*: "Everybody is bewildered at such a time."
In **almost any** *painful situation*: "This must be very difficult for you."

If you never come to the point where you feel comfortable with what to say, the rule of thumb is to say nothing and continue to let your feelings show through your silence, body language, eyes, or touch. Attentive presence may be the best you can do, but it will make no small contribution toward helping the bereaved heal.

Keep in mind, too, that the most mundane matters can intrude on and disrupt the grieving process. You can stay alert to what practical assistance might be needed and offer to take little worries off their hands like getting food in the house, making phone calls, driving to the mortuary, and taking care of the kids.

A reminder: There are problems with telling them, "If you need anything at all, please call." You can say instead, "Perhaps there's something I can do." You might try to think of things that you would need help with were you in their place, and ask, "Would you like me to call anyone?" As you leave you may want to say, "Please let me know of things you think I might be able to do. I'll call you, or you call me." If circumstances in your own life don't allow you to stay with them or follow up, it may help to say, "I'm sorry I'm not able to do more."

The moment may come when you feel uncertain as to what is wanted, and your uneasiness can get in the way of being fully present. If you begin to feel anxious, you can clear the air: "Would it help if I did such-and-such, or so-and-so?" "Would you like me to stay or would you prefer I go?" You do not need to stand around worrying about what is wanted. You can ask.

You also can inject beauty into the picture by giving your grieving friends something you think they would like: flowers, a plant, a meal, a dessert, or a special treat. You can make them feel cared for with the gift or loan of a book or a work of art, or a CD of a favorite musical piece. Nature, art, food, and drink—all can be sources of nourishment, renewal, and support.

Depending on your relationship, it may be fitting to offer consolation and wisdom from your religious tradition. It's not always easy, however, to discern what insights will bring comfort and be received as support. And when the bereaved are numb from intense grief, they usually cannot appreciate deep sentiments anyway, and you'll be wasting your sincerest efforts.

It may help to realize you do not need to defend the fantasy that life always makes sense, attempting to explain an untimely death as somehow acceptable or getting God off the hook. In the wake of a random tragedy, the bereaved may ask, "Why?" Since you don't have an answer, an honest response, which also will draw you close to them is, "I don't know." At the least, if needed and appropriate, you can reassure them that any unrelated behavior on their part did not cause the tragic death.

It also may be worth noting that the gods religions bring to our post-modern world are not in the protection business. They do not keep us safe. Not one of them. The most devout among us suffer the common cold, earthquakes and hurricanes, stock market crashes and automobile accidents, in exactly the same way as the most profane. And none of us is protected from dying. If the deities of our religious traditions don't engage in protection, perhaps we're not supposed to, either.

So if you're religious, even as you refuse to try to save your friends from their grief, you can listen sensitively with compassion and patience. Yes, if they ask you to share your faith, you can do it briefly, keeping sensitive to what encourages and supports their grieving. But more importantly, you can let your loving deeds, rather than words, declare your faith and offer consolation. And if you support the bereaved in the ways I describe above, you will represent to them the presence of a God who cares. At such painful times—as at any time—you offer friends the most healing support when you show them in practical ways that you share their pain and care about them simply for who they are.

The bereaved are bearing one of the most devastating experiences of life. They need to grieve at their own pace. If we let them express their sorrow fully and openly, they ordinarily will do it in their own time and their own way. We help by letting them take their own measured time, not by pushing. They will mend when surrounded by our patient, caring presence, not our control. Clinicians contend that when we allow people their own pace, we enhance their healing and mental health. On the other hand, if we impose our own deadlines, they may bury their negative feelings, and those suppressed emotions not only will stifle their ability to function well, but one day will take a toll on their health.

When people suffer the death of loved ones, they do not immediately lose a sense of them. The deceased continue to occupy their thoughts for some time, as if they were away on vacation and still alive. So as time goes by, rather than being part of a benign *conspiracy of silence*, you can encourage the bereaved to reminisce about the deceased, to recall their loved one's weaknesses and strong points, to recollect both sad and happy times. If you knew and appreciated the deceased, from time to time you can share with them your memories and sense of loss: "I thought of Fred the other day and how he always laughed at himself. I still miss him." To be reminded of their loved one in an affirming way supports their important commitment to the painful but important reality with which they must learn to live.

Retelling the circumstances and details that surrounded the death is another way people mourn and work through their grief. Of course, such reminiscing ordinarily will be done at memorial services or informal gatherings where memories and feelings are shared. But sensitively handled, one-on-one recollections also can play a part in moving them toward closure and full acceptance of the death.

It's also important to realize that the process of

grieving usually goes on longer than it appears on the surface and, of course, that some days for the bereaved are more dreary than others. As time goes by, and as a holiday, birthday, or anniversary of a loved one's death approaches, an empathic call can be healing: "I suspect the next few days may be very hard. Just want you to know I'm thinking of you."

You rightly are concerned, of course, if the grieving of your friends goes on endlessly. When a prolonged, dark period of sorrow does not abate, and the bereaved themselves express frustration with the slow pace of their recoveries, you might ask them to consider seeing a professional counselor or joining a bereavement support group. Hospitals usually can put you in touch with these resources. But keep in mind that our society generally expects survivors to get over their grief too quickly. Their friends often expect them to recover from a loved one's sudden death in three to six months, while experts tell us a year or two is more realistic. And when survivors have been psychologically dependent on as well as emotionally attached to the one who dies, it may take several years for the presence of the *absence* of the one who died to take a less prominent place in their consciousness. The idea is to project a realistic time frame, and not to put pressure on the bereaved simply because the pace of their grief makes you feel uncomfortable.

YOU KNOW HOW TO SUPPORT THOSE IN PAIN

You support those in grief by your full presence. As natural extensions of this commitment, you also can:

- Offer physical touch suited to the moment and your relationship.
- Empathize with their loss and their pain.
- Volunteer to assist with practical concerns.
- Clear the air when you are feeling awkward.
- Try to bring them beauty or nourishment in some suitable form.
- Share your religious insights if they ask.
- Encourage them to mourn on their own schedules.

Every encounter with grief is difficult because it has its own social context, timing, personalities, nuances, unpredictable elements, emotional intimidation, and personal demands. As with all dynamic processes, therefore, you must adapt sensitively to each situation, feeling your way based on what you discern will provide solace and healing. If the bereaved are so depressed or distraught they are out of control and threaten to harm themselves, it may be fitting to offer temporary protection, and at times it may be appropriate to involve their physicians or the police. But ordinarily you will do best to keep protection to a minimum and offer **maximum support**.

THREE POSTSCRIPTS

1. PROTECTING CHILDREN

Nice people tend to overprotect children. We ordinarily do not talk or read about death and dying to them—we're afraid of being grim or gruesome; we're afraid we'll hurt them and they'll be upset and cry. So when someone dies, we often ask children to leave the room, or we talk in hushed tones so they cannot hear the terrible news.

When we must inform them, we employ the same means to protect them we use with adults. We offer the brave front, advice, euphemisms, and religious platitudes. (Nice people have been heard to say such things as "God loved your daddy so much He has taken him to Heaven with Him.") We tend to confuse children by invalidating their pain in this way. We also distance them from us and from dealing with the hard truth of what has happened:

> A nine-year-old's favorite uncle dies on the operating table. She gets the message she will never see him again. The news crushes her. She wants to cry and scream. But all the adults around her, including her parents, say nothing to her while they tough it out. She never sees any of them cry. And she wonders what is so wrong with her for all the aching sadness and anger she feels.

Just like adults, children need to respond in healing ways to the death of someone important to them. We assist them when we offer, if possible, some indication of the seriousness of the situation before the death occurs. When a person important to them is critically ill and dying, for instance, you can prepare them for the pending event. Whenever you tell children about the death of a loved one, you do best to be brief, simple, direct, factual, and honest. Explain things the best you can in basic, physiological terms:

> As you know, Uncle Fred was very sick with cancer. The doctors did what they could to make him well, but after a while they couldn't do any more. Uncle Fred's body was unable to fight his

illness any longer, and so he died. We are all sad about it and we're going to miss him a lot.

Because children have trouble understanding what death means, and because of the disorienting shock and pain they experience, you may need to repeat what you tell them several times. It also is important to provide them with room to cry, express their feelings, and ask questions. If they have been dependent on the one who dies, they may need repeated reassurance that other adults will be there for them and loving care is not going to stop.

It does not serve children to overprotect them. They need, instead, your full presence and sensitive support that allows them to grieve and mourn in their own ways. They may grieve at a slower pace and in different ways than adults, and at special times and only in the presence of those with whom they feel safe. But they do grieve, their defense mechanisms usually enabling them to deal with no more than they can bear at any time. Children under seven, in particular, interpret what has happened in their own way and absorb only what they can handle. To broaden their experience of mourning they may want to participate in family rituals related to the death. But you serve them well if you do not force them to do so or make them feel guilty if they choose not to join in.

Sometimes, of course, older children and teens immediately grasp the significance of a loved one's death. They feel the pain deeply and become upset. When a parent dies, they often experience two losses: the parent who is gone, and the remaining parent absorbed in devastating grief. When death comes by murder, suicide, disaster, or tragic accident, particularly if it involves another child or youth, children will be especially vulnerable to confusion, anxiety, and fear and will need special attention. You can help them understand that such deaths are unusual, and, if it be the case, that they are safe and secure.

A thoughtful grandmother came to me in the year following the untimely death of her son from a terrible throat cancer. She had grieved and mourned freely, but was worried about her grandson, who seemed increasingly confused and withdrawn. She thought he might be anxious about whether he would inherit the disease. We talked about their need to talk and his requirement to feel secure. I suggested that she could say, among other things, to him, "Your daddy died from a rare tumor and we all miss him. But because he had this tumor does not mean you will have one. Your mommy and grandfather and I love you and are going to take care of you until you grow up." As they talked like this they drew closer and he became more open. She often would end their talks about his father by saying, "And you're feeling okay?" And he regularly replied, "Yes, Grandma, because I feel safe."

To support children when someone close to them dies, tell them the truth but keep your explanations to a minimum. Listen for their feelings. If they show signs of anxiety about their own safety, give them all the reassurance they need. If they fail to show any emotion at all, or continue to grieve excessively after a month or two has passed, you may be wise to seek professional counsel.

Children survive grief, as heavy as their sorrow may be, just as adults survive. Following the death of someone important to their security system, your task is to support them so they, at their own pace, can work out their feelings and come to terms with their loss. This involves having their feelings heard and accepted by family members and other loving adults. If, along with others who care, you offer them your supportive presence, you will free them to engage their grief, mourn in healthy ways, and, in the end, mature through it all.

The primary concern is to enable children to deal with their loss so it will not be buried and take a damaging toll on them later in life. If you can help them do this in the days that follow the death, you will enable them to respond well to the large and small grief-producing events they must face for the rest of their lives.

Here is the lesson: To protect children from grief is a mistake; to support them through it is to present them with a beautiful gift.

2. WHEN IT FALLS TO YOU TO BREAK BAD NEWS

A time may come when you must tell others that someone close to them has died. Circumstances will dictate where, when, how you talk to them. It may be that you must ask them to go to where the death occurred. Within whatever latitude you have, choose the best place and time to talk. If possible, speak face-to-face rather than by phone, especially if the person you must inform is alone, or if you suspect the news may be extremely devastating.

It may be valuable to have someone with you who knows as much about what happened as you do. If you can arrange this, take a few minutes together to get your bearings. Unlike the situations mentioned earlier where you arrive after the fact is known and you work at not talking right away, in these cases you have to begin by talking. Decide who will break the news, and talk about what to do if the bereaved falls apart or becomes hysterical. To complete your preparation, review your stories to see if you both understand the events the same way and have your facts straight.

Imagine that a business associate has died suddenly

at work, late in the afternoon. Efforts to reach his spouse and family by phone have been unsuccessful (she has left her work and is in the middle of a commute home). You agree, with a colleague, to go to the home and tell the family what happened. You may want to greet them with words like these:

> We need to talk with you for a few minutes, may we sit down?
> Or,
> May we come in? We're from Fred's office and need to talk with you.

After they're seated, you can tell them you're sorry, but you bear difficult news. Get to the point as quickly as possible. They will want to know important details, such as what happened, the place and time, who was present, what others did, where the body is, and who else is being notified. Here is an example:

> We can't tell you how sorry we are, but Fred collapsed in his office this afternoon about three o'clock, and apparently died immediately. [You may need to pause here, trying to sense how much is being absorbed.] The staff called 911, but when the paramedics arrived they couldn't get a heartbeat. They have taken his body to the hospital and want you to go there when you feel able.

Remember that the shock may bring tears or interruptions: "There must be some mistake!" or "You must be wrong!" or "No, it can't be!" You do not have to correct them. Be silent, letting the hard truth sink in. (If the death was by accident, suicide, or murder, or involves a child or youth, expect the loved ones to be shaken, perhaps shattered.) Try to discern what is going on in them and give them information as you think they can absorb it. After tears and the initial shock, they'll probably have questions. Listen for what they want to know. Then each time you answer a question, give them emotional *space* to formulate another question or express what they're feeling.

When you don't have answers to their questions, be honest: Tell them you don't know. Then, if it's reasonable, and you are willing to do so, offer to find out. After you have responded to questions and they still feel confused, you can try to anticipate their concerns, help them identify their options, and suggest possible courses of action for consideration.

From the start, you will put into play what we said earlier about being fully present and offering support. When you must leave, depending on their expressed needs or how you think they can function, you may need to see that someone else can be with them as a support person for a reasonable time.

3. When Grief Is Muted by Relief

With recent advances in medical science, older people in particular often linger for years before dying from debilitating illnesses. In these cases, their loved ones grieve differently from those who agonize when the one who dies is young or suffers no period of infirmity. They usually will experience in and among themselves their denial, anger, bargaining, and depression long before the day of death arrives. And on that day, rather than hurting deeply, they may be primarily relieved and ready to celebrate the end of the suffering and what the deceased meant to them.

Survivors often have been through excruciating

waiting and agonizing decisions and have real reasons to feel relieved. They may have had to watch with doctors as their loved ones moved back and forth across that difficult-to-discern but important line between **extending their living** and **prolonging their dying.** The other frustrating line that often must be faced is the one that divides the time **when the treatments are justified by the cure** and **when the treatments become worse than the disease.** During such heart-wrenching periods, they may witness their parents or friends losing their memories, abilities to communicate, bodily functions, sense of dignity, and both their reason and will to live.

And simply because of the relief they feel when the loved one dies, such survivors may find it hard to absorb the loss. It is important to assume, however, that they also are beset by negative feelings, especially guilt. Adult children may feel guilty about the care they didn't provide for their parents or their anger at having to take care of them. They may have very strong feelings about the time taken away from raising their own children, and even about their sense of relief and desire to get their own lives back to normal. It's common for people who care for dying loved ones over long periods of time to suffer mixed emotions. They can soon feel, day after day, that they can't stand it any longer, and then feel guilty about that. One of your support tasks is to help such caregivers to forgive themselves and let go of their guilt. You can watch for signs of negative feelings, confusion, and inner conflict, and then empathize:

> It makes me feel sad that you feel guilty about being relieved by your father's death. It seems normal and natural to me to feel such relief; you've been through a long, difficult time.

Or,

I don't blame you for feeling conflicted. We just don't know what to do in such situations, but you did the best you could.

Or,

I don't know anyone who wouldn't be deeply relieved. I would be.

These kinds of responses may liberate them to express their feelings without fear of criticism. Beyond that, the task is to be fully present to them and follow the basic guidelines of this chapter.

As a nice person, sooner or later life will call you to be there when someone you know must go through the pain of a loved one's death. It may be that children will be involved in the grieving. It's possible you may be asked to break the hard news to a dear friend. Or you may have to relate to those whose pain is more from confused feelings of relief and guilt, than from an actual death. You cannot save these people from their pain. And it is not in their best interest for you to try. But your refusal to be protective, your commitment to full presence, and your willingness to approach them through the caring, practical steps I have described will make them feel supported. And as a result, you'll feel more authentic as a person, you'll bring depth and breadth to your relationships, and you'll be more satisfied with your efforts at caring.

And you'll still be a *nice person*.

Author's Note

In reading this book, you've seen what it takes to liberate yourself from nine behavioral patterns and adopt healthy alternative ones. It's possible you've already let go of some of your old behaviors and now engage confidently in the new ones. Others, however, probably still stymie you. And even with your best efforts, they may take time and be hard to achieve. Sometimes personal change happens suddenly through unexpected transformation—a new insight hits you and you shout, "Aha!" It's as if you take a quick step into a beautiful sunlit room where you've never been before but that feels like home. At other times, change comes slowly through steady growth that you yourself generate by the power of your will. It's as if life is a long journey in search of your home, and you're slowly, painfully making progress toward it. Change toward maturity inevitably enriches your life, but it's not always fast or easy.

So where are you in this change process? It's a good time to take inventory. You can underline the steps you've already taken in the following checklist. Then number in order those you haven't, but want to, perhaps noting alongside them in the margin the dates by which time you want to take them.

263

( ) To accept myself for who I am, rather than try to earn my acceptance.

( ) To manage my life in balance, rather than burn myself out.

( ) To speak up, rather than stifle my legitimate interests.

( ) To express my anger creatively, rather than suppress it.

( ) To listen and empathize when attacked, rather than be defensive.

( ) To try to tell the appropriate truth when people fail me, rather than lie.

( ) To offer information to others, rather than give them advice.

( ) To encourage loved ones to save themselves, rather than rescue them.

( ) To support those who are in pain, rather than protect them.

If you're the typical nice person, even after you adopt the new behaviors, you'll lapse back into old patterns on occasion, just as I do. This needn't discourage you. When we were first learning to walk, we bumped into things and fell a lot, but it never occurred to us to stop trying. You can count it a plus that you now recognize your lapses and have creative ways to deal with them.

Whenever I suffer a relapse, I first forgive myself. Next, I reflect on how to avoid that mistake the next time I'm in a similar situation. I find growth a fascinating challenge. I also let my awareness of the lapse remind me that I'm very much alive, that learning from mistakes is important, and that both my awareness and my commitment to grow are signs I'm becoming the person I need and want to be.

I find it helpful to be reminded regularly of the various alternative behaviors. I often tell myself in the morning, "You don't need to be perfect today." I sometimes remind myself that on this day I may have to say no to a request or delegate a task to someone else. When I set up my weekly calendar, I make sure I include times to reduce stress and renew my energy. And I always try to schedule a balanced selection of immediate and long-range good times to which I can look forward.

I also prepare mentally for encounters that are potentially stressful. When I think I'll face a situation in which it's difficult to say what I want, I rehearse the assertiveness lines on pages 80–83. Not only does my anxiety usually disappear, but when the moment comes, I can express my wishes clearly and comfortably. If I think I'll meet someone who always makes me angry, I scan specific sections on pages 108–119. If I'm faced with going to people who are in grief, I think through what I need to focus on doing: listen quietly, empathize when they express pain, offer appropriate physical touch, anticipate practical problems I can help with, and so on.

MAKING THE MOST OF THE BOOK

This book can become your new behavioral handbook. Whenever you have trouble with a particular mistake, you can review the relevant chapter.

- When you're trying to prove yourself or are doubting your worth, the first two chapters will remind you that you're loved and that, indeed, in the grand scheme of things, **you matter.**
- When your feelings are blocked by fear and anger,

you can go back to pertinent sections of Chapters 3 through 6. They'll help liberate you to express your feelings constructively.

• When you find yourself leaping to save friends by controlling, rescuing, or protecting them, the last three chapters will put you back on track.

In addition, you may find it helpful to:

1. List key concepts on a blank flyleaf at the back of the book. (Our social nature, pages 3–6; accepting your acceptance, pages 18–20; being fully present, pages 76–78; etc.)
2. Summarize on a three-by-five card the steps to an alternative behavior you're working on, and carry it folded in your wallet.
3. Keep the book on your nightstand, in your backpack, or in your briefcase.

When people are frustrated by their good intentions and ask you about changes you've made, explain your choices or point them to this book. If you've learned the lessons here, you'll be content merely to describe your new behaviors. You won't need to talk endlessly about your progress or advise them that they *should* read the book. You'll be sensitive to the fact that no one deserves to be badgered by those who have *annoying virtues*.

Of course, when you master one of the alternative behaviors, it will be time to celebrate your accomplishment. You can congratulate yourself, let others admire your new skills, and, above all, enjoy what you've achieved. And as you increasingly balance your life, express your feelings forthrightly, and offer genuine support to those who are important to you, living in these integrated, healthy ways will become more natural and life will be more satisfying.

And, yes, through it all, you'll still be a *nice person*.